Weetabix®

Book of the
MILLENNIUM
Volume 3: 1701–1900

from the publishers of
The HUTCHINSON
ENCYCLOPEDIA

Helicon

Copyright © Helicon Publishing 1999
All rights reserved

First published for Weetabix Limited in Great Britain in 1999 by
Helicon Publishing Ltd
42 Hythe Bridge Street
Oxford OX1 2EP
e-mail address: admin@helicon.co.uk
Web site: http://www.helicon.co.uk

The Weetabix name and logo are the registered trade marks of Weetabix Limited.

Typesetting by Tech Type, Abingdon, Oxon
Layout and design by Norton Matrix Limited, Bath
Printed in Italy by De Agostini, Novara
ISBN: 1-85986-327-2

British Library Cataloguing in Publication Data

A catalogue record for this book is available from the British Library.

Papers used by Helicon Publishing Ltd are natural recyclable products
made from wood grown in sustainable forests. The manufacturing
processes of both raw material and paper conform to the environmental
regulations of the country of origin.

Contributors and Advisors

Ian Crofton	Susan Mendelsohn
Bernadette Crowley	Nigel Seaton
Susan Cuthbert	Cath Senker
Giles Hastings	Andrew Solway
Maggy Hendry	Lisa Sullivan
Louise Jones	Sarah Wearne
Brenda Lofthouse	Christine Withers

Editorial and Production

Editorial Director
Hilary McGlynn

Production
Tony Ballsdon

Managing Editor
Katie Emblen

Picture Research
Elizabeth Loving

Project Managers
Robert Snedden
Lisa Sullivan

Cartography
Olive Pearson

Art and Design
Terence Caven

Editors
Rachel Minay
Edith Summerhayes

Contents

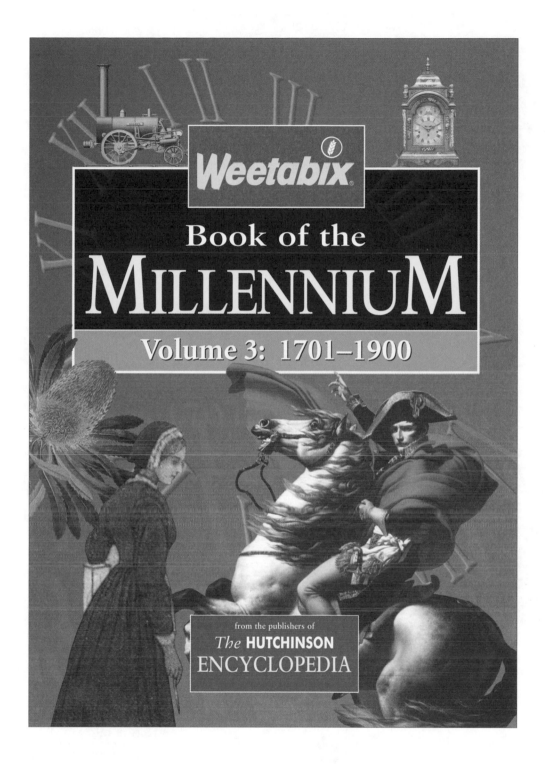

Weetabix

Book of the
MILLENNIUM

Volume 3: 1701–1900

from the publishers of
The **HUTCHINSON**
ENCYCLOPEDIA

The World 1701–1900

1776
American colonists sign the Declaration of Independence during the American Revolutionary War.

1789
A French mob storms the Bastille prison in Paris, sparking the French Revolution.

1865
The Northern states win the US Civil War.

18th century
The Enlightenment, introducing new ways of thinking, spreads in Europe.

19th century
Spanish and Portuguese colonies in the Americas gain their independence.

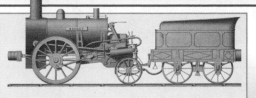

1770s

The Industrial Revolution begins in England.

1853

After more than 200 years of isolation Japan is forced to open up trade with the West and begins a period of rapid modernization.

mid-19th century

David Livingotono and other explorers travel in Africa.

1770

British Captain James Cook sails into Botany Bay and claims the whole of the east cost of Australia for Britain. The colony of New South Wales in Australia is founded to serve as a British penal colony in 1788.

1880

European powers begin colonizing Africa. By 1902 nearly all of Africa is controlled by Europeans.

The 18th-Century European Wars

The War of the Spanish Succession

King Louis XIV of France, who ruled from 1643 to 1715, wanted to make his country the superpower of Europe. In order to achieve this aim he involved France in many wars. His last great conflict was the War of the Spanish Succession, which broke out in 1701.

It started over a dispute about who would succeed King Charles II of Spain, who had died childless in 1700. Charles had willed his title to Louis XIV's grandson, the Duke of Anjou, who became King Philip V of Spain. Charles II, however, was a member of the Habsburg family, who ruled Austria and the Holy Roman Empire. The Habsburgs felt that one of their family should inherit the title.

Britain, the Dutch Republic, and the Holy Roman Empire were alarmed that Spain was now ruled by a relative of the French king Louis XIV, so they formed an anti-French alliance. Prussia, some other German states, and Portugal later joined them. Many battles were fought, with the anti-French alliance gaining more victories. However they failed to remove Philip V from the Spanish throne.

In 1713 and 1714, when France and Spain realized they were not going to win the war, they negotiated peace treaties, called the Peace of Utrecht, with the allies. Most of Spain's European empire and some French overseas

main areas of war
- War of the Spanish Succession
- War of the Austrian Succession
- Seven Years' War

territories were divided between the allies. The question of the Spanish succession was resolved. Philip V was allowed to remain king of Spain and its overseas colonies under the condition that Spain and France did not unite again.

The War of the Austrian Succession

From 1740 to 1748 a series of wars broke out in Europe, which together are known as the War of the Austrian Succession. The war started when Charles VI, the Habsburg Holy Roman Emperor and archduke of Austria died in 1740 without a male heir and his lands passed to his daughter, Maria Theresa. Two months later Frederick II of Prussia invaded Silesia, one of the richest Habsburg provinces. Prussian victory prompted the forming of an anti-Habsburg alliance that included Prussia, Bavaria, Spain, and France.

Maria Theresa refused to surrender. She agreed a truce with Prussia and attacked her other enemies. The Austrians fought successfully but Prussia came back into the conflict and won a series of victories that forced Maria Theresa to

The Rise of Great Britain

Britain became Europe's greatest power after the European wars of the 18th century. France surrendered to Britain all its Canadian territory and its lands east of the Mississippi River in North America. The French also gave up most of their territory in India. Spain surrendered Gibraltar and Minorca (both strategically important) to Britain. Spain also gave Britain sole rights to the slave trade in the Spanish colonies in the Americas.

Maria Theresa, one of the greatest of the Austrian Habsburg rulers.

give up control of Silesia to Frederick II in 1745. Maria Theresa retained control of Austria however and secured the Holy Roman Empire for her husband, Francis I, who became Holy Roman Emperor that year.

Also in 1745 the French won a tremendous victory over a combined army of Austrian, British, and Dutch forces at the Battle of Fontenoy in the Austrian Netherlands. However French success in Europe was overshadowed by the loss of much of their Canadian territories to Britain.

The war was concluded in 1748 by the Treaty of Aix la Chapelle.

All the pre-war territorial agreements in Europe were restored with the exception that Prussia kept hold of Silesia. This gain in wealth and population brought Prussia up to the level of the great European powers. The conflicts between Britain and France over their overseas colonies were not settled, however, and the treaty did not bring a lasting peace.

The Battle of Fontenoy in 1745, at which the French won a great victory.

The Seven Years' War

In 1756 the Seven Years' War broke out, which began as a continuation of the quarrel between Prussia and Austria over Silesia. New alliances were formed – Prussia was joined by Britain, while Austria was joined by France, Sweden, and Russia. Prussia, not helped much by Britain in the beginning, won many great battles but by 1761 had become exhausted from fighting on two different fronts. However, in that year Peter III, an admirer of Frederick II, became tsar of Russia and withdrew from the war. Austria could not defeat Prussia alone and a treaty confirming Prussia's control over Silesia was signed in 1763. Meanwhile, in North America and India the French and British were fighting for control. These wars ended with victory for Britain, confirmed by the Treaties of Paris in 1763.

The Enlightenment

A scientific revolution had taken place in Europe in the 16th and 17th centuries. The new discoveries of such men as Copernicus, Galileo, and Isaac Newton gave people a better understanding of the universe. This was based on logical reasoning and not on old ideas. The rise of modern science inspired a new way of thinking that came to be called the Enlightment.

The great scientist Isaac Newton was one of the major influences on the thinkers of the Enlightenment.

The Scottish Enlightenment

Scotland was an important centre of Enlightenment thinking. In the 18th century Scotland had more universities than England, and they were responsible for many advances in science, medicine, philosophy, and economics. The two most famous thinkers of the Scottish Enlightenment were David Hume and Adam Smith. David Hume was a philosopher and historian who questioned many existing ideas and showed that virtually no 'truths' about reality can be proved by logical reasoning. His most famous work is *A Treatise of Human Nature* (1739–40). Adam Smith helped to change economic thinking in his great book *The Wealth of Nations* (1776). In this he argued for free trade (no taxes on imports and exports) and for governments not to interfere with business.

Deism

Reason (the power of the mind to think and understand) became more and more valued as a means of discovering truth. Reason was applied to religion. The search for a 'rational' religion came up with deism. Deists said that God is the creator of the universe but is not involved in the lives of humans and does not make miracles. They rejected all the teachings, rules, and rituals of organized religion, and hated religious intolerance. Some thinkers went even further and dropped the belief in God altogether, claiming that there was no evidence to prove his existence.

Independent Thought for All

The spread of printing made information easily available to all. People felt that they could use their minds to work out, discover, and describe the truths for themselves. They felt freed from the chains of superstition, secure in their own ability to understand.

Society began to be viewed not as a part of God's order, but as an arrangement between human beings for the good of all. The idea of 'the social contract' became important – an agreement entered into by all members of a society to benefit all. This idea had first been developed in the 17th century by the English philosophers Thomas Hobbes and John Locke. In the 18th century the Frenchman Jean-Jacques Rousseau took this idea further in his book *The Social Contract* (1762).

This movement towards independent thinking, 'common sense', and reason occurred all over Europe in the 18th century. Superstition, intolerance, brutality, and the authority of the church and state were all attacked. In Britain this movement was called 'the Enlightenment', and similar terms, all involving light, were used in other countries.

The Influence of the Enlightenment

The Enlightenment left a lasting imprint on Western society. Some rulers, such as Frederick the Great of Prussia, Joseph II of Austria, and Catherine the Great of Russia, were inspired by Enlightenment ideas when they introduced reforms in their countries. The emphasis of Enlightenment thinkers on the equal rights of all members of society were largely ignored by these and other rulers in Europe, however, and certainly contributed to the French Revolution of the late 18th century. The American Revolution of 1776 also had its roots in Enlightenment thinking. However, towards the end of the century some people began to believe that reason was not the only way to the truth. This was the beginning of the Romantic movement, which stressed the importance of emotion and imagination.

A Revolution in Farming

Great advances were made in farming in the 18th and 19th centuries. This 'Agricultural Revolution' started in Britain, and spread to other countries in Europe, and to North America. In order to feed a growing population, people began to think of ways to redistribute the land and to use it more efficiently. New machines were invented that could do the work better, faster, and cheaper than people or animals. While fewer people were needed to work on the land, more and more people were needed to work in the factories of the Industrial Revolution. There was a great migration of people to the growing towns and cities, and by 1850 there were more people living in towns in Britain than in the countryside.

The Enclosure Movement

In medieval Europe peasants would farm narrow strips of land scattered among fields around their lord's manor. Similar systems of farming were used in China and Japan. In the 15th century land owners in England began to enclose their land with hedges, converting cultivated land into pasture for sheep. Later enclosure movements, especially in the 18th and 19th centuries, allowed land owners to grow the same crop over large areas of land. This was more efficient than farming on narrow strips and it allowed farmers to develop better crops and farming techniques. However, enclosures caused great suffering to many ordinary peasant farmers, who were forced off the land. In Ireland and the Scottish Highlands, for example, many people were evicted from their land during the 19th century, and many were forced to leave their countries.

A steam-driven plough is demonstrated in 1857.

Commons

In Britain and the USA, commons are areas of public land. They started out in England as parts of a lord's property that he did not use for farming. The commoners who lived on his land and worked for him would be allowed to use the 'common' area to let their animals graze. Today commons are mostly used for sports and relaxation. Some examples are Clapham Common in London, England, and Boston Common in Massachusetts, USA.

Technology in Farming

The Industrial Revolution in the 18th century brought new machines that made life easier for farmers.

1701	Jethro Tull designs his seed drill for planting.
1831	Cyrus McCormick invents a mechanical grain reaper, a machine for cutting grain.
1836	A combination harvester-thresher is patented. An early combine harvester, it is pulled by a horse.
1837	John Deere begins making steel ploughs.
late 19th century	Steam power increasingly replaces animals to run machines on farms.
1892	John Froelich builds the first petrol-driven tractor.

A painting showing Jethro Tull demonstrating his new invention, the seed drill.

New Farming Techniques

Once the fields were enclosed, animals could be kept apart, and farmers could select the best animals to breed. This produced healthier, larger animals. Farmers also began to grow crops such as turnips to feed animals through the winter. Before this, most animals were killed in the late autumn, and the meat salted to preserve it. Now fresh meat was available all year round.

Farmers began to experiment with new ways of rotating the crops so that their land could produce more food. In four-field crop rotation, a different crop was grown on each field in turn. Typically the crops were winter wheat, turnips, spring barley, and clover. Clover, which could be grazed by cattle, gave back nutrients to the soil, and meant that the field did not have to have one year lying fallow (not growing anything, to allow the soil to recover).

Domestic pigs were very different from their slimmer wild relatives.

Jethro Tull (1674–1741)

Jethro Tull was born in Berkshire, England, in 1674. He went to Oxford University and trained to be a lawyer, but never practised law and decided to run his father's farm in Oxfordshire instead.

Jethro was a great musician, and liked to play the organ. In 1701, inspired by the design of the organ, he designed a drill with a rotating cylinder that he could use in farming. The machine was pulled by a horse and planted seeds in neat rows. Before this machine, called a seed drill, farmers would scatter seeds by hand.

In 1709 Jethro bought a farm of his own and made more advances. By pulverising (crushing) the soil between his rows of seeds, he was able to get air and water to the roots and so did not need to use manure for fertilization. In 1731 he published a book that described his new tools and methods, called *The New Horse Hoeing Husbandry*. Many methods of modern farming are based on his ideas.

John Deere (1804–1886)

John Deere started his career at 17 as an apprentice to a blacksmith in Vermont, USA. In 1837 he moved west to Illinois and produced the first steel plough. His ploughs became very popular, because they were able to cut through the hard soils of the North American Prairies. This turned the Prairies into the greatest wheat-producing region in the world. By 1857 Deere was producing more than 10,000 ploughs a year. His company was amazingly successful and by the end of the 20th century it was the biggest farm-equipment manufacturer in the USA.

The American Revolution

Washington crossing the Delaware River in his retreat from New York.

The Causes of the Revolution

In the 18th century there were 13 colonies ruled by Britain on the east coast of North America. The colonists did not have any representatives in the Parliament in London, and many felt that they should govern themselves. They did not like some of the British laws, such as the Navigation Acts, which said that all trade with the colonies had to go by Britain. The colonists were even

NORTH AMERICA

Saratoga
Lexington
Bunker Hill
Boston
New York
Yorktown

✗ battle
☐ 13 Colonies

George Washington (1732–1799)

George Washington was the great-grandson of an English settler. He was born in Virginia and was a land surveyor before the Revolution. He also fought in the colonial army with the British against the French. In 1789 he was elected first president of the United States of America and served two four-year terms.

angrier when the British government decided to tax the colonists for the first time in their history.

In 1765 Britain passed the Stamp Act, which taxed newspapers and documents used in the colonies. This angered the colonists so much that in 1766 the taxes were stopped. Shortly afterwards another law was passed obliging the colonists to provide food and shelter for British troops. In 1767 Britain raised further taxes on everyday goods. In 1773 Britain passed the Tea Act. The colonists saw this as an attempt to make them drink taxed tea. A whole shipload of tea was thrown into Boston harbour in what became known as the 'Boston Tea Party'. The British then closed the port of Boston and made stricter laws for the colonists.

The War Begins

In 1774 the colonies joined together and formed a Continental Congress (a kind of parliament) and drew up an appeal to King George III and the people of Britain – although at this stage they did not demand independence. The British responded by sending more soldiers

The Declaration of Independence

On 4 July 1776 the American Congress passed the Declaration of Independence. It was written by Thomas Jefferson and said that the united colonies were free and independent states. Representatives of all 13 states signed it. The 4th of July is still celebrated in the USA as a public holiday.

British Redcoats

British soldiers in America were nearly always at a great disadvantage. Most men wore bright red long-tailed coats, which earned them the nickname 'redcoats'. These coats made the soldiers easy targets for the colonists, who often preferred to fight from covered positions and not out in the open as soldiers did in Europe.

The Boston Tea Party

On 16 December 1773 groups of colonists, disguised as Mohawk Indians, boarded three ships in Boston harbour. They threw the cargo of tea overboard to show their hatred of the tax put on them by Britain. Other ports decided to have 'tea parties' of their own. King George III was outraged and ordered Boston to be closed until the tea and tax were paid for.

to America, and the colonists began to assemble arms at Concord and Lexington. In April 1775 the British commander General Gage sent soldiers to seize these weapons and the first shots of the Revolution were fired. The first major battle took place at Bunker Hill where the colonists proved that they could match the British soldiers, known as redcoats. Congress then appointed George Washington as the commander in chief.

In 1776 Congress issued the Declaration of Independence, and in the same year Washington was forced to retreat by General Howe, who took New York. In 1777 the British decided

that if Washington's army could be defeated then the war would end. General Burgoyne would attack from Canada and join up with Howe to crush Washington. The plan failed, and Burgoyne was surrounded and surrendered at Saratoga. Britain had other enemies in Europe and this defeat brought them into the war on the colonists' side. The fleets of France, Spain, and the Netherlands outnumbered the British and made it hard for supplies and reinforcements to reach America. However, the British had several successes in the south under Lord Cornwallis. He occupied Yorktown but became trapped by Washington's army and by French ships at sea.

In October 1781 Cornwallis and his 7,000 men surrendered. Although a British army was still in the north, the British government decided that it was time to end the fighting. In 1783 a peace treaty was signed in Paris, and Britain recognized the independence of the United States of America, as the former colonies now called themselves.

The French Revolution

In 18th-century France there were three Estates, or classes of people. The First Estate was made up of members of the church. The nobles, who owned about one third of the land, formed the Second Estate. The Third Estate (or Commons) included everyone else – peasants (farm workers), workers, and middle-class people such as lawyers and doctors. The Third Estate paid most of the taxes but had no part in running the country.

In the 1780s the people of the Third Estate were angry. The middle classes wanted a share of power. The peasants were starving because harvests were bad. Between April 1788 and March 1789 bread became one and a half times more expensive, and there were riots. Meanwhile, King Louis XVI was spending more money than he could raise.

In 1789 Louis XVI called a meeting of all the Estates, the States-General, hoping to ask the First and Second Estates to pay more taxes.

The 1789 Revolution

The king wanted the three Estates to meet separately. The middle-class leaders of the Third Estate insisted they all meet together. The Third Estate declared their assembly to be the National Assembly. Now working people also wanted a share of power so they took to the streets in demonstrations. On 14 July 1789 they took over the Bastille prison in Paris to show their strength. By October food had become scarce. A crowd, mostly of women, marched from Paris to Versailles to bring the royal family to Paris and to demand bread. In the countryside peasants attacked the homes of rich landowners.

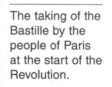
The taking of the Bastille by the people of Paris at the start of the Revolution.

War with Austria and Prussia, 1792

France went to war with Austria and Prussia because they were plotting to return Louis XVII, the son of the executed king, to power. France also hoped to spread revolution to other countries; its message was 'war on castles, peace to cottages'. The French turned back the Prussian–Austrian forces, but there were no revolutions elsewhere in Europe.

Women in the French Revolution

Many middle-class women campaigned for the same rights as men. In 1789 Olympe de Gouges wrote the Declaration of the Rights of Women, saying, 'All women are born free and remain equal to men in rights'. Working women in towns were more worried about bread prices. It was mostly women who took part in bread riots.

The execution of the king of France on the guillotine.

The Republic, 1792

In 1791 a new constitution (a set of rules saying how a country should be governed) was formed. It said that the government, and not the king, had the power to make laws. Some people, called Republicans, did not want a king at all. In 1792 armed people attacked the Tuileries, where the king and his family were living, and took them to prison. A new government, called the National Convention, was set up and established a republic. People who were thought to be enemies of the new republic were executed on the guillotine, a device for chopping off heads. In January 1793 the king himself was beheaded. Many ordinary people were pleased. Mercier, a Convention member, described it this way: 'His blood flows; cries of joy from 80,000 armed men fill the air'.

The Reforms of 1789

The National Assembly made changes that helped the middle classes but did less for the workers and peasants.

- Feudalism (peasants giving landlords taxes and working for them without pay) ended.
- All jobs were open to the Third Estate.
- The justice system became less brutal.
- No taxes were charged on goods sold within France.
- The government took church land and sold it, keeping the money.

A crowd of people burn the symbols of monarchy in the Place de la Concorde, Paris.

The Declaration of the Rights of Man, 1789

The slogan of the French Revolution was 'Liberty, Equality, Fraternity'. The new government after the Revolution developed these ideas in the Declaration of the Rights of Man, which said:

- All men are born free and equal.
- All men are subject to the same laws and taxes.
- All men have the right to own property.
- All men have the right to say what they like in public and in newspapers.
- All men are free to practise any religion.

From The Terror to the Fall of Napoleon: France 1793–1815

Naploeon Bonaparte, who effectively ended the revolution when he declared himself emperor.

Maximilien Robespierre, who became associated with the worst outrages of 'The Reign of Terror'.

The Terror

In 1793 a political group called the Jacobins took power in France, led by Maximilien Robespierre. They were middle-class reformers who had been involved in the Revolution, and they had the support of many poor people. The new government threw its enemies into prison, and 17,000 people were sent to the guillotine. Rebellions in Lyon and the Vendée region were cruelly put down. This period became known as 'The Reign of Terror'.

Napoleon Bonaparte (1769–1821)

Born in Corsica, Napoleon went to school in France and joined the French Army. He turned into one of the most brilliant generals the world has ever seen. In 1796 and 1797 Napoleon took over northern Italy for France and fought the British in the Middle East. He went on to win decisive victories over the Austrians, Prussians, and Russians.

Napoleon was a clever ruler who would pay any price for success. After a series of defeats in 1814, however, he was pushed out of power. Yet he gathered together a new army, returned to Paris, and set up his empire again in 1815. He stayed in power for 100 days before being defeated at Waterloo.

In 1794 food prices rose and there were riots. The Jacobins did not help the Paris poor, and lost their support. People in the government now turned against Robespierre for taking too much power for himself. When he tried to speak in the Convention in July they cried 'Down with the Tyrant!' Robespierre was arrested and sent to the guillotine.

The Directory 1795–1799

The government was now run by a group of five men called the Directory. Poor people had little influence, and rich people felt they could show off their wealth again. The Directory was weak. In 1795 the army, led by Napoleon Bonaparte, protected it against rebels who wanted to have a king again. In 1799 Napoleon took power from the Directory.

France under Napoleon

Napoleon made sure that he had every part of France under his control. He drew up a new set of laws called the Napoleonic Code. In 1804 he made himself emperor of France. He asked the Pope, head of the Catholic Church, to crown him. At the last moment Napoleon grabbed the crown and put it on his head himself.

Napoleon formed a new group of nobles – princes, dukes, and barons – and gave them land so they would support him. Yet he was cruel towards his enemies, who were thrown into prison. Just like the kings of France, Napoleon kept all power for himself.

The new ruler put great efforts into making the French empire bigger. Yet once he started losing wars, the French people turned against him and he finally fell from power in 1815 and the monarchy was restored.

The Revolutionary and Napoleonic Wars	
1792	Austria and Prussia invade France, but are defeated. France conquers the Austrian Netherlands (present-day Belgium).
1793	Britain and other European countries declare war on France.
1796–1797	Napoleon wins many victories in Italy.
1798	Napoleon is defeated by the British at the Battle of the Abukir Bay.
1800	Napoleon defeats the Austrians at Marengo, Italy.
1802	Britain and France make peace.
1803	War breaks out again. Napolean plans to invade Britain.
1804	Napoleon makes himself emperor.
1805	Nelson defeats the French at the Battle of Trafalgar, ending French plans to invade Britain. Napoleon turns east, and defeats the Austrians at Ulm and the Austrians and Russians at Austerlitz.
1806	Napoleon defeats the Prussians at Jena. The French are now masters of Germany.
1808	Napoleon makes his brother king of Spain. Spanish guerrillas, aided by British troops, begin to fight the French.
1809	The Austrians are defeated, and join Napoleon's side.
1812	Napoleon invades Russia, but is forced to retreat in winter, losing most of his army.
1813	The French are defeated in Spain at Vitoria, and in Germany at Leipzig.
1814	British troops enter France. Napoleon is exiled to Elba, a small island off the coast of Italy.
1815	Napoleon returns to France, but is finally defeated by the British and Prussians at Waterloo.

✗ battle

☐ French empire

☐ area ruled by Napoleon's family

☐ state dependent on France

Transport: Roads, Canals, and Locomotives

In the early 18th century transport had changed little since the Middle Ages. Most roads were rutted and muddy. On the better roads, people had to pay fees called tolls. Slow, horse-drawn carts carried heavier loads, while faster, more comfortable carriages carried passengers. The cheapest way to move large loads was by boat.

New ways of making iron in much larger amounts were being developed, and the first steam engines had been built. Iron and steam were the first steps towards the Industrial Revolution. But before the Industrial Revolution could really begin, a transport revolution was needed.

Roads, Canals, and Trackways

Large amounts of coal were needed for fuelling steam engines and making iron, so roads and waterways had to be improved to move coal from mines to the foundries where iron was

made. The engineer Pierre Trésaguet, who became inspector general of roads in France in 1775, did much to improve road construction. In Britain, Thomas Telford and John McAdam made improvements of their own, and soon there were good, paved roads in many parts of France and Britain.

More important for moving heavy materials were canals. Britain had few canals in the mid-

The Rainhill Trials

The Liverpool to Manchester railway was the first mainline railway to be built. In 1829 the line was nearly complete, and the owners held a competition at Rainhill to find the best locomotive for the new line. The task was to haul a load of 20 tonnes 15 times along a kilometre (2 mile) track, at a speed of 16 kilometres per hour (10 miles per hour) or faster. Three locomotives took part: the *Novelty*, the *Rocket* and the *Sans Pareil*. The *Rocket*, designed by George Stephenson and his son Robert, was the only locomotive to complete the task successfully. It reached a speed of nearly 50 kilometres per hour (30 miles per hour) with a full load.

The construction of Hampstead road bridge.

18th century, but from about 1760 engineers such as James Brindley began building a network of canals to provide a cheap way of moving coal. In some hilly areas, however, canals were almost impossible to build. To haul coal in such places, trackways were laid, carrying wagons with special wheels.
The wagons were either drawn uphill by horses or lowered downhill using gravity.

Steam Power on Land

It was not long before someone thought of using steam power to pull wagons along these trackways. Steam engines had been in use since the end of the 17th century for pumping water out of mines, and in the 1760s the Scottish engineer James Watt invented a much more efficient type of steam engine. Then, in 1802, an English mining engineer called Richard Trevithick built a light, high-pressure steam

The building of the stationary engine house for the railway at Camden Town, London.

engine that could run on a trackway. This was the first steam locomotive. Another English engine-builder, George Stephenson, improved greatly on early locomotive designs. In 1825 his engine the *Locomotion* pulled a train carrying 450 passengers from Stockton to Darlington. This was the first public passenger-carrying railway.

The new railways were enormously successful. The first mainline railway was opened between Liverpool and Manchester in 1829. Other lines soon followed in Britain, Europe, Russia, and North America. By the end of the 19th century there were nearly a million miles of railway lines around the world.

Steam carriages were built in the early 19th century, but it was in Britain in the 1830s that steam power on the road was most successful. For about ten years steam-powered carriages built by Sir Goldsworthy Gurney ran on several routes, carrying many passengers.

railway built by 1836
railway built between 1836 and 1852

17

Transport: Steamships, Bicycles, and Cars

The *Natchez* and the *Eclipse* race along the Mississippi River at night.

Steam Power at Sea

While Richard Trevithick and George Stephenson were building locomotives in the early 19th century, other engineers were putting steam engines in boats. The earliest boats were driven by paddle wheels. There were experiments in France and Britain in the late 18th century, and the first commercial steamboat services began in the USA in 1790. By 1830 there were 200 paddle steamers on just the Mississippi. As railways began to be built in the 1850s, however, river steamboats became less important. Engineers turned their attention to developing ocean-going steamers.

Atlantic Crossings

The first steam crossing of the Atlantic Ocean was made by the *Savannah*, a US ship, in 1819. The *Savannah* was actually a sailing ship that also had a steam engine. Steam power was used for less than 90 hours of the 29-day voyage. In 1838, the British engineer Isambard Kingdom Brunel turned his attention to steamships. He realized that the larger a ship was, the more

Isambard Kingdom Brunel (1806–1859)

Isambard Kingdom Brunel was one of the great British engineers of the 19th century. His father, Marc Brunel, was also an engineer, and Isambard began his career working for his father on constructing a tunnel under the River Thames linking Rotherhithe with Wapping in southeast England. In 1833 Isambard was made chief engineer for the Great Western Railway, and this became one of his greatest projects. He designed the track, the engines, bridges, and tunnels – even the lights in the railway stations.

After designing the *Great Western* and the *Great Britain,* Brunel planned an even larger ship – the *Great Eastern.* This gigantic vessel was 211 metres (692 feet) long, and no larger ship was built for 40 years. It was designed for long-distance passenger voyages, but the company building it went bankrupt and the ship was used instead to lay the first transatlantic telephone cable.

18

efficient it would be. The result was the *Great Western*. Larger than any other ship of its time, it could carry passengers and cargo across the Atlantic. It was so reliable that it soon began regular passenger services, the first ship to do so.

In 1843 Brunel designed a truly revolutionary new ship, the *Great Britain*. The hull was made of iron instead of wood, and the ship used screw propellers instead of paddle-wheels. Once again it was the largest liner in the world at the time – 98 metres (322 feet) long, and weighing over 3,000 tonnes.

Petrol Power

By the mid-19th century a new type of engine, much lighter than the steam engine, was being developed. It was called the internal-combustion engine, and it used coal gas for fuel. Two Germans, Karl Benz and Gottlieb Daimler, were the first to put these lighter

Bicycles

Bicycles first appeared on the roads In the 19th century. The first bicycle with pedals was built in 1839 by a Scottish blacksmith, Kirkpatrick Macmillan. Then, in the 1860s, the French Michaux brothers built a much more popular design, in which the pedals were attached to the front wheel. To improve their speed, these bicycles were built with a large front wheel and a much smaller back wheel. In Britain they were known as 'penny-farthings'.

In 1879 Harold Lawson built a bicycle with a chain from the pedals to the back wheels, and in 1885 the first Rover safety bicycle was built, with all the main features of the modern bicycle. Today bicycles are the most widely used form of transport in the world.

A penny-farthing rider looks set for a painful landing!

engines on wheels. Benz built a lightweight three-wheeled car, which he first showed in Paris in 1885. The car was beautifully made and sold well, and by 1888 Benz had 50 craftsmen working for him.

Gottlieb Daimler and another engineer, Wilhelm Maybach, built a more advanced engine than Benz's. It could run much faster, and it had a carburettor, which allowed the engine to run on petrol instead of coal gas. In 1885 Daimler put an engine into a bicycle, and in 1886 he built the first four-wheeled car. Within ten years factories all over Europe and in North America were making cars.

Karl Benz and some of his friends in one of the cars he invented.

19

The Industrial Revolution: Brand New Machines

In the 18th and 19th centuries there were great changes in the way goods were produced. Instead of people making things on a small scale at home, they started to make them in much larger numbers using big machines in factories. This was called the Industrial Revolution.

Canals were an important part of the transport network that supported the Industrial Revolution.

Why did the Industrial Revolution begin in Britain?

There were several reasons why Britain was the first country to industrialize. Britain had plenty of natural resources such as coal and iron. Transport had improved, with new canals and better roads. Farming methods were also improving, so there was enough food for the growing population. Also, Britain was a wealthy country, enjoying peace with its neighbours.

The Cloth Industry

For many centuries woollen cloth had been made in Britain. In the 18th century the cotton cloth industry began to develop. At first, people spun and wove the cotton at home. Then new machines were invented that could make the cloth much faster. Over ten times more cotton was being produced in 1830 than in 1760. The machines were big and expensive, and it became easier to make cotton and woollen cloth in factories than in people's homes.

Workers could no longer make a living producing wool or cotton at home – they could not work as fast as the machines.

James Watt (1736–1819)

Born in Greenock, Scotland, James Watt was ill as a child, and instead of going to school he learnt many skills in his father's engineering shop. It is said he was fascinated by steam at a young age. He was often told off for wasting time watching the kettle lid rising and falling as the water boiled.

At 18 James went to Glasgow and then London to train to be a maker of scientific instruments. In 1763 he was given a Newcomen steam engine to repair, and realized he could make a better engine. He invented one that used only a quarter of the coal needed by earlier engines, and was more powerful. In 1775 Watt went into business with Matthew Boulton to build steam engines. They built the first steam engine to drive factory machinery in 1782. Watt carried on working on new inventions until his death.

A full-size working model of Hargreaves's spinning jenny.

New Inventions for Making Cotton			
Date	Invention	Inventor	What it did
1733	Flying shuttle	John Kay	Wider pieces of cloth could be woven more quickly.
1765	Spinning jenny	James Hargreaves	16 threads could be spun at a time instead of 1.
1769	Water frame	Richard Arkwright	Spinning machine driven by water power; it could only be used in a factory.
1785	Power loom	Edmund Cartwright	Loom driven at first by water, later by steam power.

The First Factories

In the late 18th century factories were built near rivers, because they used power from water wheels. Richard Arkwright built the first water-powered cotton factory in Cromford, Derbyshire, in 1771. At first people did not want to work there. Working in a factory meant that they had to work fixed hours, because all the machines started and stopped at the same time. Arkwright built houses, a church, and an inn to attract workers. In the end, more than 5,000 people worked at Cromford.

James Watt's first design for a locomotive engine.

The Steam Engine

The earliest types of steam engine were built by the Englishmen Thomas Savery in 1698 and Thomas Newcomen in 1712. James Watt started work on improving Newcomen's steam engine in the 1760s, resulting in a much more efficient engine that turned wheels to drive big machines. The steam engine was probably the most important invention of the Industrial Revolution. It was more powerful and reliable than water wheels, which did not work if the river dried up or froze.

The number of steam-powered factories grew very quickly during the early 19th century. The invention of the steam engine also led to the growth of many other new industries.

The Industrial Revolution: Workshop of the World

After the steam engine was invented to drive machinery, it was used in many industries. These included iron and steel, shipbuilding, and the railways.

Iron and Steel

Iron was used for building steam-powered machinery, railways, ships, and bridges. There was a great need for it during the Industrial Revolution. In 1709 Abraham Darby showed how coal, baked into coke, could be used to smelt iron. This was a method of crushing and heating rocks containing iron. It worked much better than smelting with charcoal from wood. In 1784 Henry Cort found out how to make iron stronger, and 20 years later four times as much iron was being produced.

In 1856 Henry Bessemer showed how to make large amounts of steel for half the cost. Steel was firmer and stronger than iron, but could be shaped easily. In the 1870s railway makers and shipbuilders changed from using iron to steel.

Coal

Vast amounts of coal were needed to fuel steam engines. Miners had to dig deeper and deeper underground to find it. Mining was a dangerous business, but some inventions made it easier. After 1775 a steam-powered pumping engine made by James Watt was used to drain the water from deep coal mines. In 1815 Sir Humphry Davy invented a safety lamp that would not set fire to the gases in mines, as candles had done. Even so, miners often carried a canary to warn them of gas. The bird would die before the gas exploded.

Workshop of the World

By 1850 Britain was the most powerful industrial country in the world. It became extremely wealthy by making natural materials like cotton and iron into goods that were then sold for a lot of money. Britain became known as the 'Workshop of the World'. After about 1850 ordinary working people's lives started to improve, although they still had to work incredibly hard. Between 1850 and 1864 the average national income per person rose by one-third. This was a time when Britain was very confident. However, by the 1870s other countries had built up their own industries and were starting to compete with Britain.

Children in the Mines

Many boys and girls worked in the coal mines because they were small enough to walk through the narrow tunnels. They had to push and pull huge baskets of coal along in the dark. The youngest children, aged between five and ten years old, worked as 'trappers'. They opened and closed underground doors to allow the baskets through. From 1842 children under ten years old and women were not allowed to work underground in Britain.

The Great Exhibition of 1851 was a spectacular display of Great Britain's wealth and power at that time.

The Industrial Revolution soon spread to Europe. These furnaces are in Germany.

The Iron Puddler

The most important iron worker was the puddler. He stirred the iron in the furnace (a kind of large oven) to burn off the bits that were not pure. His work was difficult and dangerous, and the furnace was incredibly hot. Iron puddlers in Sheffield in the late 1860s lived to an average age of only 31.

Life and Work in Towns and Factories

Living in Towns

In 19th-century Britain many people moved from the countryside to towns to work in the factories. By 1851 more than half of the people lived in towns. This was a major change.

Most working people lived in overcrowded slums that were close to the factories. Their homes were tiny, cheaply built, and packed together. Few had gardens. There was no running water indoors, so people had to fetch water from a pump or pipe outside in the street. The dirty water they simply threw out of the window.

Victorian writer Elizabeth Gaskell described the dirty homes: 'The cellar in which a family of human beings lived was very dark inside. Three or four children were rolling on the damp, nay wet, brick floor, through which the stagnant [still and smelly], filthy moisture of the street oozed up.'

A young boy is shown mending shoes in this late 19th-century photograph.

Factory Life

By 1839 there were over 400,000 factory workers in Britain. Of these, nearly half were under the age of 18, and over half were women and girls. Factory life was extremely hard. People worked up to 14 hours a day, 6 days a week. They began at about 6 a.m., and had only short breaks for breakfast and lunch. The factories were usually noisy and crowded, and often too hot in summer and too cold in winter. There were no toilets – mostly there was just a bucket in the corner for everyone to use.

Everyone had to work fixed hours. The factory bell rang to tell the workers when to start and finish work. Some people worked at night and had to sleep during the day. Families used to say that the beds

Factory Reforms

Government reforms made factory life a little easier.

1833 Factory Act: Children under 9 were not allowed to work in factories.

1844 Factory Act: Women and children under 18 were not allowed to work more than 12 hours a day.

1847 Ten Hours Act: A 10-hour day was introduced for women and children under 18.

Children in Factories

Before the reforms many children worked in factories for up to 16 hours a day because their families needed the money. The working conditions were harsh and the work they had to do was hard. They had to crawl under machines to oil them or to clear away rubbish. This was dangerous – sometimes they were caught in the machine and hurt. If they worked too slowly or fell asleep they were beaten.

Inside a typical 19th-century cotton mill.

Community activities were encouraged in Robert Owen's New Lanark.

never grew cold, because they were often shared. Someone was always just getting up as another person was going to bed.

Many women went to work in the new factories. This meant they earned their own money and had some independence. But they worked such long hours and were always so tired that they had little time to enjoy themselves.

Robert Owen (1771–1858)

Robert Owen was born in Wales and started his career as an apprentice in a clothing shop. In 1800 he took over New Lanark spinning mill in Scotland. He treated his workers well, building good houses for them and giving them better wages for shorter hours than normal. Owen thought little children should not work, and set up the first infants' school in Britain. In 1825 he set up a cooperative (sharing) village in the USA called New Harmony, where people shared work and food equally. Unfortunately, they argued and it failed. All his life Owen supported cooperatives and trade unions.

Sickness and Health

In the 18th century most people in Britain lived in filthy homes with no running water. They did not realize that it was important to wash to stay healthy. People would throw their rubbish out of the window or into rivers. Diseases spread quickly in the crowded streets.

A French military surgeon of the early 19th century does what he can for those wounded in battle.

Doctors knew little about treating diseases. Only the poor went to hospitals, which were dirty and crowded. Often they died from infections there.

18th-Century Improvements

During the 18th century doctors learned more about how the body works and how to treat some illnesses. Between 1700 and 1800 more than 100 new hospitals were built in Britain. Until the mid-18th century, operations were done by barber-surgeons, who knew nothing about medicine. In 1746 a Scottish surgeon, William Hunter, started teaching his pupils about the body. He and his brother John changed surgery 'from a trade into a science', even though it was still extremely dangerous.

In 1796 Edward Jenner found a way to protect people against smallpox, a disease that killed large numbers at that time. He discovered that people who were exposed to the much milder disease cowpox did not get smallpox. He deliberately gave an 8 year old boy cowpox and

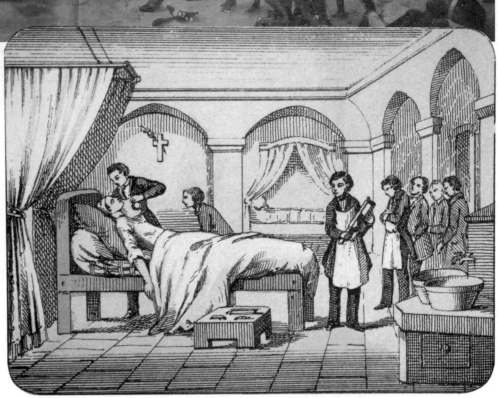

A patient is given ether to make him unconscious before surgery is carried out.

Anaesthesia

The 19th century saw the introduction of anaesthesia – the use of drugs to put the patient to sleep so they would not feel pain. Anaesthesia was pioneered by two Americans, Horace Wells, who used nitrous oxide (laughing gas), and William Thomas Green Morton, who used ether. In Britain anaesthesia using chloroform was introduced by the Scottish surgeon James Simpson.

An operation usually involved cutting off a part of the body, such as an arm or leg. This was extremely painful, as there were no drugs for putting the patient to sleep. The person was often given lots of brandy to drink, and the surgeon tried to operate as quickly as possible. The surgeon probably wore dirty, old clothes because people did not know that germs caused infection. The tools – saws and knives – were not kept clean either. Patients often died afterwards from an infection. Surgeons did not enjoy their job; one 18th-century surgeon, John Abernethy, was almost always sick when he did an operation.

Safer Childbirth

In the mid 1840s Hungarian doctor Ignaz P. Semmelweiss reduced the death rate of women after giving birth from 30 per 100 to 1 per 100, by insisting that childbirth wards were kept clean and germ-free. His ideas were not taken seriously until after his death, when Louis Pasteur's theory that germs cause disease became accepted.

Nuns have a long history of caring for the sick. The first hospitals were in nunneries and monasteries in the Middle Ages.

then a few weeks later exposed him to smallpox. The boy did not develop the disease. This was the first vaccination, exposing a person to a mild form of a disease so they develop resistance to a more dangerous form.

Sickness and Health in the 19th Century

During the 19th century many people moved to towns to work. Health conditions were worse than in the countryside. Working people were packed together in tiny homes. Many illnesses, such as cholera, were carried by dirty water. Cholera swept across Britain in 1831 to 1832 and in 1848, killing rich as well as poor people. Slowly the government began to pass laws making people responsible for cleaning up the towns. In 1875 the Public Health Act set up committees in each area. These had to provide clean drinking water, sewage systems (to take away dirty water), and clear away rubbish. There were also improvements in treating illness. From 1858 doctors had to be trained. In the 1850s and 1860s the French chemist Louis Pasteur developed his theory that germs cause disease. In 1865 the British surgeon Joseph Lister found out how to kill germs to protect his patients from infections. By 1900 clean water and sewers had helped to save many lives, and medical treatment was much safer.

Average Ages of Death in 1842

	Manchester (town)	Rutland (county)
Professional people	38	52
Farmers and tradesmen	20	41
Mechanics and labourers	17	38

From Government Commission Report on the Sanitary Conditions of the Labouring Population, 1842

Life in Britain: At Home

A wealthy family of the early 18th century.

Homes

In the 18th and 19th centuries many people still lived in the countryside. Rich people had large, beautifully decorated country houses full of paintings and expensive furniture. They had gardens and parks with lakes and fountains. Poor people, such as farm workers, lived in two- or three-roomed cottages made of stone, or wood if they lived near a forest. Their homes had low ceilings and small windows without glass. They were often damp and cold.

During the 18th century many rich people built themselves elegant houses in town centres. As towns grew bigger and more crowded, they moved to the edges of towns instead, and poor people moved into the town centres. In the19th century working people lived in tiny houses

Children's Clothes

Wealthy little boys wore dresses until they were about five years old, and sometimes had long hair. This was called 'being in petticoats'. When they were a little older they wore short trousers. Once they were about 10 they wore the same kind of clothes as their fathers. Girls wore dresses like their mothers', but with shorter skirts. At 15 they started to wear long dresses and tie up their hair.

Poor children usually had second-hand clothes, called 'hand-me-downs'. Often they had no shoes. They might tie straw or sacking around their feet to keep them warm. In the 19th century little boys were often seen wearing a hat, but no shoes.

Clothes and Fashion

Poor people usually had only one set of clothes. They wore clothes that were right for the kind of job they did. For example, women coalminers wore padded trousers. Male farm workers wore hard-wearing breeches (short trousers) and smocks (loose overalls). For the rich, fashions changed often. Here are some typical fashions for the rich:

1730s Gentlemen: long coat with a high collar, worn open; knee-length breeches; powdered wig; three-cornered hat.

1780 Ladies: high powdered wig with ribbons and feathers on a wire frame; full satin skirt, stretched over a hoop fan.

Early 19th-century Gentlemen: riding costume (top hat, tailcoat, tight trousers, and riding boots).

1810 Ladies: silk bonnet; thin, close-fitting dress with high waistline.

Mid-19th-century Gentlemen: big bow tie; frock coat; watch chain; fancy waistcoat; patterned trousers; moustache.

1850s Ladies: crinoline (a wide frame under the dress).

Late 19th-century Gentlemen: plainer clothes, including a shorter jacket, with matching trousers and waistcoat.

A working class family home of the late 19th century.

Food

Poor people cooked on an open fire in the corner of the room. In rich homes there was a separate kitchen, and the cooks and servants made the food. Iron stoves came into use in the early 19th century, but at first only wealthy people had them.

Wealthy people ate meals with several courses. They started with soup and fish, followed by two kinds of meat and vegetables, and pudding afterwards. At dinner parties they would enjoy many kinds of fish and meat, drinking a different wine with every course.

Poor people had very plain food. The English ate a little meat, made into broth (soup), and mostly bread and potatoes. In Ireland people lived mainly on milk and potatoes, and in Scotland oatmeal porridge with milk was the normal food. The poor drank ale (beer), or sugary tea. Between 1720 and 1750 gin was popular in England. It was cheap, but dangerous because it was so strong. One advertisement said 'Drunk for a penny, dead drunk for twopence'.

close to the new factories. After 1834 the poorest people with no money had to move to workhouses, where men and women were kept apart. Husbands were separated from wives, and sisters from brothers. In the workhouse they lived and worked with many other poor people in horrible conditions.

A Victorian family enjoy a day out at the seaside.

Leisure Time

Most people had little time off work, just Sundays and church holidays, such as Christmas. Sometimes there were special events, like a fair, with dancing shows, boxing matches, and swings to ride on. In the 19th century railways were built. By the end of the 1840s ordinary people could afford to buy a third-class train ticket and visit the seaside for the day.

Life in Britain: At School

Before 1870 many poor children did not go to school. Country children worked in the fields with their parents. In towns they helped at home or worked in factories. Few rich girls went to school. A governess (woman teacher) taught them subjects like reading, sewing, and French at home. They learnt music and dancing from a tutor (private teacher). Rich boys often went to expensive public schools such as Eton or Rugby when they were about ten years old. They learnt Latin and Greek, and played lots of sport.

School Reforms

1844 Factory Act: children working in factories had to go to school six half days a week.

1862 Teachers' pay depended on how well the children had learned during the year. (This was stopped in 1897.)

1870 Elementary Education Act: all areas had to provide schools for 5–12 year olds.

1880 All children aged 5–10 had to go to school.

1891 Board schools were made free for all children.

1899 Children had to go to school until age 12.

Lessons at a Board School

Lessons were boring by modern standards. The teacher stood at the front of a class of up to 80 pupils writing words or sums on the blackboard. The children copied them on little boards called slates. Most of the time pupils learnt reading, writing, arithmetic, and religion. Boys would do some woodwork while girls did cooking. For PE children mostly marched round and round the playground swinging their arms.

A Victorian girl sits at her writing desk.

Teachers and pupils in the courtyard of Eton College in the early 19th century.

Church Schools

In the 18th century well-off people set up many small charity schools for poor children. The churches opened Sunday schools, and by 1851 over 2 million children went each week to learn to read the Bible. The churches also set up weekday schools called National, or British, schools. At these schools, one teacher taught some facts to a few older children, called monitors. The monitors then repeated these facts to the younger children, who would repeat then over again to try to learn them.

Dame Schools and Ragged Schools

Dame schools were run by women who taught up to 20 children squashed into a room at home. Some dames could not even read themselves!

One of the ragged schools where poor children were given a free education.

There were also ragged schools in some towns, where poor children could learn for free. In Scotland parish schools taught poor children.

In 1841 a Parliamentary Commission showed that most children could not read or write and knew very little about the world. They met boys who had never heard of London. One young miner, when asked who Jesus was, said, 'Does 'e work down the pit?' The government decided children would grow up to be better workers and sensible voters if they all went to school.

Board Schools

The government passed a law in 1870 saying that there should be school places for all 5–12 year olds. In areas where there were not enough schools, new 'school boards' were set up. A similar law was passed in Scotland in 1872. It was cheap to go to a board school, and extremely poor children did not have to pay at all. Even children from workhouses, where the poorest people with no home or money lived, could go to board schools.

31

Queen Victoria

Victoria was 18 when she became queen in 1837. Although this was young to be a queen, the politicians were amazed at her confidence when she read out her first speech. The Duke of Wellington said, 'She not merely filled her chair, she filled the room.'

Osborne House on the Isle of Wight where Victoria spent much of her time.

Prince Albert

Victoria met Prince Albert, her German cousin, in 1839. Afterwards she wrote in her diary, 'Albert really is quite charming, and so extremely handsome ... my heart is quite going'. They married in 1840. Prince Albert helped Victoria to do her government work and run the royal household, and Victoria came to rely heavily on her husband.

Disraeli and Gladstone

In 1861 Prince Albert died and Victoria became deeply depressed. In the 1870s Benjamin Disraeli, the Conservative prime minister between 1874 and 1880, encouraged Victoria to be seen in public again. Victoria liked Disraeli greatly. Disraeli wanted to make the British Empire even bigger, as did Victoria. He charmed the queen by paying her compliments. In 1876, with Disraeli's help, the government agreed to call Victoria 'Empress of India', which was then ruled by Britain.

Victoria hated William Gladstone, who was the Liberal prime minister four times between 1868 and 1894. Gladstone brought in many reforms that Victoria did not like. He changed the way education, the legal system, and the army were run. For example, the commander-in-chief of the army was to answer to Parliament rather than to the queen.

Later Life

In the early 1880s several of Victoria's close friends and relatives died, including her daughter Princess Alice, Disraeli, and her devoted servant John Brown. These deaths saddened her greatly, but in 1886 she became active in public again. In 1887 she celebrated 50 years' rule at her Golden Jubilee; her Diamond Jubilee was in 1897. During the Boer War in South Africa (1899–1902) she visited the returning troops and gave out medals. Victoria died in 1901.

Victorian Architecture

Before the Industrial Revolution each part of the country had its own style of building, using local materials. In the 19th century, it became cheap to use large amounts of iron, glass, and bricks. Similar kinds of buildings could be built all over the country.

Victorian architects copied the Gothic style that had been popular in Europe from the mid-12th century to the 16th century. This style was used for churches and for public buildings such as Manchester Town Hall. Engineers also used new styles and methods of building. Iron was strong and long-lasting. The Crystal Palace, built for the Great Exhibition of 1851, was a giant construction of iron and glass. Gardner's Warehouse in Glasgow was made of iron too.

Victoria's reign was an important period for building, from homes to railway stations and large public buildings that were used for running Britain and its vast empire.

The Royal Albert Hall in London, built in 1871 using profits from the Great Exhibition that had been organised by Prince Albert in 1851.

Classical Music and Impressionist Art

Classical Music

The Classical period in music lasted from about 1750 until about 1830. Classical music was formal and carefully balanced, and the same musical structures were used for many of the pieces. At the start of the period most musicians worked either for the church or for a rich patron. But soon new audiences of wealthy people became interested in music and were willing to pay to hear a concert. This made it possible for a musician to make money without having just one patron. The great composers of the time, mostly based in Vienna, in Austria, were Haydn, Mozart, and Beethoven.

In the Classical period many forms of instrumental music were developed. Symphonies (long orchestral pieces) developed from the overtures that orchestras played at the start of an opera. Haydn wrote over 100 symphonies for his patron, Prince Esterházy.

The young Mozart (seated) plays with his father and sister. He was only five when he wrote his first symphony.

Chamber music (music for small groups of instruments) was also important in this period. The most popular grouping was the string quartet of two violins, viola, and cello. There were also many pieces for the piano, which was then a new instrument.

Classical Opera

Early in the Classical period opera was divided into two styles: the noble, serious *opera seria* and the light-hearted *opera buffa*, or comic opera. *Opera buffa* often poked fun at serious opera, and took its stories from everyday life. In the later 18th century composers such as Gluck began to reform *opera seria*, making it simpler and more dramatic. Some of Mozart's operas, such as *Idomeneo*, are in the *opera seria* style. Some of his most famous operas, such as *Don Giovanni* and *The Marriage of Figaro*, are in the *opera buffa* style, but with more feeling.

Inside an 18th-century opera house.

A painting by Renoir - *Dance in the City.*

Many classical works were written in four sections, or movements. The first movement was fast but serious, followed by a slow, stately movement. The third movement could be a graceful minuet (a kind of dance) or a lively scherzo (which means 'joke'). Last came a brilliant, fast finale.

New Styles of Art

Romanticism
Romanticism was a late 18th-century and early 19th-century movement in art and literature that emphasized the imagination and emotions of the individual artist. Romantic painters, such as J M W Turner and William Blake, often drew their inspiration from nature and the past.

Impressionism

Impressionism was a style of painting developed by a group of French painters in the late 19th century. They rejected conventional styles of painting that tried to make everything look realistic, and instead tried to catch an impression of the play of light and shadow in a scene at the time they were painting. Famous Impressionists include Claude Monet, Pierre-Auguste Renoir, and Edgar Degas. They achieved the shimmering style of their paintings using dabs of different colours, side by side. Impressionism was the first great revolutionary movement of modern art.

Post-Impressionism

In the 1880s and 1890s a variety of styles, known collectively as Post-Impressionism, followed the Impressionist movement. Post-Impressionist painters tried to go beyond the Impressionists' concern with light and shadow. Underlying shapes and forms and subject matter became more important. Famous Post-Impressionist painters include Vincent van Gogh and Paul Gauguin.

Protest and Reform in Britain

In the 18th century changes were being made to people's lives without their permission, so they protested to make their voices heard. Poor people protested about low pay and high food prices, especially after 1750. There were more than 700 riots between 1793 and 1815. From the 1790s people rioted and smashed machinery, because the new machines in the factories made goods more cheaply than people could at home, and many craftspeople became unemployed. From 1811 until about 1816 a group called the Luddites damaged cloth factories in many parts of northern England and the Midlands.

Huge demonstrations were held to protest about the treatment of six workers from Tolpuddle, Dorset, who were sent to Australia in 1834 for forming a union.

Early Trade Unions

From 1824 workers were allowed to group together in trade unions to protect their rights and fight for better pay and working conditions. By 1834 there were more than 800,000 people in trade unions. The first big trade union was the Grand National Consolidated Trades Union (GNCTU), formed in 1833 by mill owner Robert Owen. The union claimed that 500,000 people joined, but still the government managed to crush it after arresting some of its members.

Political Reform

In the early 19th century there was a campaign to change the voting system. Many people had

The Reform Acts

1832 Number of voters up from 440,000 men to 657,000. New industrial towns got MPs, and places where few people lived lost MPs.

1867 Every house-owning man could vote; this was one in three men.

1884 More than 2 million more men could vote, including farm workers. No women could vote.

William Cuffay (1788-1870)

William Cuffay, son of an ex-slave, was a tailor. In 1839 he joined the Chartists. He organized protest marches and was an excellent speaker. In 1848 Cuffay was arrested for helping to plan a rebellion. At his trial he said this was not true, but still he was sent to Tasmania, Australia, as a punishment. He carried on working for political rights in Tasmania and stayed there for the rest of his life, even though he was pardoned in 1856.

moved from the countryside to the towns. Yet some large new towns, such as Sheffield and Manchester, had no members of Parliament (MPs). The 1832 Reform Act gave more men the vote, and the new towns gained MPs.

Chartism

Working people were unhappy with the 1832 Reform Act because they did not get the vote. The Chartist movement, set up in 1838, wanted working people to have some power in Parliament, and wrote a 'People's Charter' to list their demands. The Chartists organized petitions to support their demands in 1839, 1842, and 1848. The first had over a million signatures. But Parliament did not agree to the demands. Some Chartists held demonstrations to try to persuade Parliament to listen, but these failed too. In 1848 the Chartists were forced to give up.

A cartoon of the time shows the Chartists delivering their demands to Parliament.

Trade unionists marching through Manchester in support of farm labourers in 1874.

New Unions

From the mid-19th century new unions were set up for skilled workers – people with a trade, such as engineers and carpenters. The first women's trade union was started by sewers in Edinburgh, Scotland, in 1872. Then unskilled workers – who had no special trade – also formed trade unions. In 1888, 1,400 women at the Bryant and May match factories in London went on strike for better pay and conditions, and won. It was the first strike by unskilled workers to win, and other successes followed.

However, by the end of the 19th century low-paid workers still had no say in government. In 1900 the Labour Representation Committee (later renamed the Labour Party) was set up to give workers a voice in Parliament.

1848: Revolution in Europe

What Started the Revolutions?

In 1848 a series of revolutions broke out across Europe. There were many reasons for this. One was the poverty that most people suffered. Crop failures had led to famine (food shortages) in some countries in the 1840s and unemployment was high.

The kings and queens of Europe, who lived in splendour, did little to help their people. These monarchs usually had total control over their countries. Rich people – especially the nobles – and the clergy also had some political influence, but most people had no say in their country's government.

Many countries did not have their own rulers, but were ruled by another country. The emperor of Austria controlled an empire that included northern Italy, Hungary, and what are now the Czech and Slovak Republics.

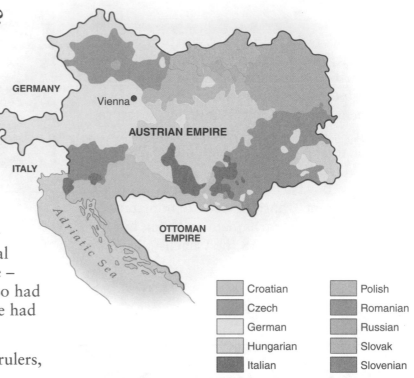

▨ Croatian		▨ Polish	
▨ Czech		▨ Romanian	
▨ German		▨ Russian	
▨ Hungarian		▨ Slovak	
▨ Italian		▨ Slovenian	

Angry protestors at the French Chamber of Deputies in February 1848.

Prince Klemens von Metternich (1773–1859)

From 1809 to 1848 Prince Klemens von Metternich served as an important minister in the Austrian government. He was so powerful that the period he held office is often called the 'Age of Metternich'. During the early 19th century liberal and nationalist movements spread across Europe. Metternich was strongly against these movements, and used spies across Europe to tell him of any political threats. He not only protected the Austrian empire, but also used his influence to support other European monarchs against the unrest of their people. When he was forced from office in 1848 he fled to England. Even though he returned to Austria after the revolutions, he never held office again.

Italian troops fight to win their independence from Austria.

Who Started the Revolutions?

Most of the revolutions were started by people from the educated middle classes. There were various political movements in Europe in the 1840s. One of these was called liberalism, a movement that called for personal freedom, social progress, and for the people of a country to have a say in their government.

The first major rebellion in 1848 took place in France in February. People demanded voting rights and protested against corrupt governments and unemployment. The French king, Louis Phillipe, was forced to give up his throne.

Effects of the Revolutions

Some positive changes were achieved by the revolutions. Shocked by the uprisings, monarchs began listening to calls for more liberal forms of government. In France the right to vote was achieved. One of the biggest changes was the end of manorialism in parts of Germany and Austria. Manorialism was a system in which peasants were dependent on a rich landlord. The landlord owned a manor, or estate, on which the peasants lived and worked. In return for their work, the landlord fed, clothed, and housed them. However, the peasants had few or no rights. The liberation of the peasants meant they could own land and work for themselves.

The next uprising occurred in Vienna, the capital of the Austrian empire. The rebellion drove the very powerful Austrian minister Klemens von Metternich from office. Shortly afterwards violent protests erupted in other parts of the empire as different nationalities within the empire demanded the right to control their own affairs.

Within the year, however, all the rebellions had been put down. Arguments between the different political groups weakened the rebellions. Armies, who had stayed loyal to the monarchs, received orders to crush any uprisings with brute force. Monarchies were restored everywhere except in France, where the revolution had some success. Despite their sudden end, however, the 1848 revolutions led to positive changes in many countries that would come later in the century.

The Rise of Nationalism

The 1848 revolutions introduced the idea of nationalism to many countries. Nationalists think that people should look to their nation, or country, to meet their social, economic, and cultural needs. With nationalism a sense of belonging is felt by people who have the same language, religion, and traditions. Before nationalism people rarely felt part of an entire nation. Instead they looked to their church, tribe, village, or ruler to meet their needs and to help them feel a sense of community.

Karl Marx

Who was Karl Marx?

Karl Marx was a German revolutionary, philosopher, and economist, the founder of a body of ideas called Marxism. With Friedrich Engels, he wrote much of the theory of Communism. This theory put forward the idea that everyone was equal and that property should be owned in common. Members of the community would see to each other's needs.

Marx lived in the 19th century, a time of great change in Europe. The Industrial Revolution was taking place, which changed the economy and the lives of many people. Before, most people had lived on the land, working as farmers. Now, large numbers of them became workers in factories.

What did Marx Say?

Marx said that the world was divided into two classes of people: the ruling class and the working class. Ruling-class people owned property – the land and the factories. They were rich. Working-class people did not own property and had to work hard for a living. They were usually poor.

Marx believed there would be a huge struggle between the classes. The workers, grouped together in large numbers, could join together in a revolution to overthrow their bosses and then could run society for themselves. The wealth of industrial society could be shared out fairly among people, according to their needs. But this would only happen if the workers all over the world organized themselves together to change their lives through revolution.

Karl Marx (1818–1883)

Karl Marx was born in 1818 in Trier, Germany, to a comfortable, well-off family. His parents were Jewish, but his father had converted to Christianity. In 1835 Marx went to Bonn University to study law. Here, he got drunk and ran up debts. The following year he moved to Berlin University and became interested in philosophy.

In 1843 Marx married Jenny von Westphalen and they moved to Paris, where Marx became a revolutionary. After being thrown out of France, Belgium, and then Germany, Marx and his family settled in London in 1847. They lived in terrible poverty, and three of their six children died. Marx's great friend Friedrich Engels helped the family to survive. In the 1860s Marx worked hard on *Das Kapital,* although he was ill. After the collapse of the Paris Commune in 1871, Marx spent his last years quietly studying.

What did Marx Do?

Marx also took part in political activities. In 1847 he and Engels wrote the *Communist Manifesto* for an international workers' party, the Communist League. In 1848 there were revolutions all over Europe, creating great excitement among revolutionaries. However, they were all crushed. Marx returned to writing, starting work on his economic theories. These theories were explained in his four-volume work *Das Kapital* which was published between 1867 and 1895.

In 1864 Marx helped to set up the International Working Men's Association, later known as the First International. It was a union of independent organizations of working people. In 1871 Marx was very encouraged by the Paris Commune, a revolutionary uprising of workers in Paris. Yet when the uprising was put down, there was a campaign against the First International, and arguments among its members. Marx disbanded the organization in 1876.

A group of workmen in London in 1870.

The front cover of the Manifesto.

The Communist Manifesto

The Manifesto of the Communist Party (1848) was written by Marx and Engels to state the policies of the Communist League. It says that the history of all society is the history of class struggle between the rulers and the people they rule. One day, the working people will take control of society. The Communists will lead them because they understand what needs to be done to overthrow society. The aim is a new society in which 'the free development of each is the condition for the free development of all'.

The Manifesto ends with the words: 'The workers have nothing to lose but their chains. They have a world to gain. Workers of the world, unite!'

The Crimean War

From 1853 to 1856 a war was fought in the Crimea, a peninsula on the northern shore of the Black Sea. The Crimea was then part of the Russian empire. The war began when Russia invaded territory belonging to the Turkish Ottoman Empire, and the Turks declared war on Russia.
The Ottoman Empire, whose territory included southwestern Europe and the Middle East, was once very powerful, but in the 19th century the empire was decaying.

- ✕ battle
- Russian land
- land gained from Turks
- Turkish lands

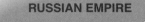
RUSSIAN EMPIRE

Crimea

Sevastopol

Black Sea

Constantinople

OTTOMAN EMPIRE

Alma River

Sevastopol — Inkerman

Balaclava

A photograph of the harbour at Balaklava in 1854. This is one of the first photographs taken during a war.

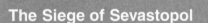

The Siege of Sevastopol

The biggest operation of the Crimean War was the siege of Sevastopol – the main base of the Russian navy on the Black Sea. About 50,000 French and British troops, plus 10,000 Italian troops from Sardinia-Piedmont, which joined the war in 1855, besieged Sevastopol for 11 months in 1854 and 1855. The Malakhov fortress in Sevastopol had excellent defences, which the allies could not break down. The winter months of the siege caused terrible suffering among the allies. Their generals had not ordered enough food, water, or clothing for the troops, resulting in thousands of deaths. The siege ended when the Russians evacuated the fortress in 1855.

Florence Nightingale (1820–1910)

The British nurse Florence Nightingale volunteered to go to the Crimea to nurse the soldiers when she heard about the terrible state of the British hospitals there. They were filthy, infested with rats, had little food, and were short of bandages and beds. When Florence arrived in the Crimea with 38 nurses she took control of all nursing activity at the war front. She had kitchens and laundries installed in the hospitals and worked almost round the clock. The wounded soldiers called her 'the lady with the lamp' because she walked the wards with a lamp during the night to make sure everything was under control.

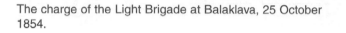

The charge of the Light Brigade at Balaklava, 25 October 1854.

Britain and France, two of the biggest powers in Europe, feared that Russia might have plans to conquer the entire Ottoman Empire. Not only would this make Russia dangerously powerful, but also if the empire was to fall Britain and France wanted a share of its territory themselves.

The first battle took place on the Black Sea. It was fought between the Russian and Ottoman fleets, and the Russians won. In 1854 Britain and France decided to support the Turks. They declared war on Russia and sent ships to the Black Sea. In September 1854 the British and French landed troops in the Crimea and attacked the Russian naval base at Sevastopol. Other major battles were fought that year at the Alma River, Balaklava, and Inkerman.

In September 1855 the French successfully stormed the Malakhov fortress in Sevastopol, a major Russian stronghold. At this point the Russians decided to withdraw from the Crimea. They blew up their fortresses, sank their ships, and evacuated Sevastopol. However, Russia

The Charge of the Light Brigade

One of the most famous military blunders in history – the Charge of the Light Brigade – occurred in 1854, during the Crimean war. It happened because the British general of the Light Brigade received muddled orders. He commanded his cavalry to charge along a valley to attack a Russian artillery unit stationed at the end of the valley. Unknown to the British, Russians were also positioned on high ground along the length of the valley. As the Light Brigade charged, Russians fired at them from three directions. Of the 673 men who started the charge, 110 were killed, 134 were wounded and 45 were taken prisoner.

continued fighting the war elsewhere. When Austria threatened to help the Turks, Russia accepted the peace terms of the Treaty of Paris in March 1856.

The Crimean War has gone down in history as 'the war that shouldn't have happened'. While the conflict took place it became clear that neither side could win. Troops endured terrible suffering – approximately 250,000 men were lost by both sides. More men died of disease than during the fighting, because of severe weather conditions, a shortage of food and water, and poor medical care. The war did have a significant effect on the future of Europe, however, where important changes took place within the next decade.

Armies and Navies

Had a military man of the early 18th century been able to see two centuries into the future he would have been astounded. To his eyes, the early 20th-century armies and navies would seem massive in size and extremely well trained. Transport, battle strategies, and weapons would have changed beyond recognition.

Men were often forced against their will to join the navy by press gangs.

Workers inside the Woolwich Arsenal.

Conscription

Through most of history, soldiers fought in times of war, then returned home when the conflict ended. By the 18th century warfare had become so common that many European countries wanted larger, more permanent ('standing') armies. They used conscription to force men to join their ranks. In this way Frederick the Great, the king of Prussia from 1740 to 1786, increased the size of his army from 90,000 to 150,000 men soon after he was crowned. Many of the conscripts constantly watched for opportunities to escape, and at one battle 16,000 men deserted. By 1813 Prussia had a much more effective conscription system, which created a large standing army backed by even larger trained reserves. This became the model for most European countries. However, both Britain and the USA only used conscription during major wars, otherwise relying on a smaller, professional army.

Children at War

It was not unusual to find children as young as eight years old in European armies during the 18th century. Boys could join the navy at ten or eleven years old as officers' servants. Some were called 'powder monkeys' because they had the dangerous job of carrying cartridges of explosive powder to the cannons during a battle.

Lord Nelson (1758–1805)

The English admiral Horatio, Viscount Nelson, was born in Norfolk, England, the sixth of 11 children. His uncle, Captain Maurice Suckling, took the young Nelson to sea. His genius as a commander was not immediately recognized, but by 1800 Nelson had become a national hero in Britain. The people idolized him for his victories at war and his humane behaviour as an officer. Many historians consider Lord Nelson's triumph at the Battle of Trafalgar in 1805 to be the greatest victory in the history of the Royal Navy. It forced Napoleon to give up his dream of invading Britain once and for all. But the gunshot wounds Lord Nelson received in the battle proved fatal, and he died on 21 October 1805. His final words were, 'Thank God, I have done my duty'.

Iron and Steam

The Industrial Revolution gave Western Europe and the USA advanced transport, ammunition, and many other items needed by armies and navies. Iron and steel were used for bridges, railways, and guns. Iron warships powered by steam replaced wooden-hulled sailing ships, and steam-driven railways sped supplies and men over large distances. New tools were devised for making faster, more accurate guns. An Englishman known as 'Iron-mad Jack' invented drills that made it easier to build accurate cannons and rifles. A US inventor named Eli Whitney opened a gun factory where individual gun parts were made separately by machines and then put together. This was the beginning of modern mass production.

Food Supplies

Between 1701 and 1900 the population of the world grew rapidly, and so did the size of its armies. One reason for this was food. New farming methods and machines produced much bigger crops – and they were needed. The daily requirements for an army of 250,000 men and 100,000 horses were 225 tons of bread, 550 tons of oats, 550 tons of hay, 450 tons of straw, and 2,800 tons of fresh fodder. As the great French general Napoleon said, 'An army marches on its stomach'.

The Slave Trade in the Americas

The Reasons for the Slave Trade

By the 18th century European countries such as Spain, Portugal, and Britain had taken over many parts of the Americas as their colonies. They realized that they could make much money from mining and from growing crops on big plantations, but they needed a huge number of people to do the work. A highly profitable trade grew up, in which Europeans bought millions of slaves in West Africa and took them across the Atlantic Ocean to work in the Americas. The slave owners grew rich quickly.

Conditions on slave ships were appalling with people chained together and crammed into every available space.

They forced the slaves to work extremely long hours and did not pay them. Slaves also worked as household servants and craftspeople.

Life as a Slave

Slave life was incredibly hard. Slaves had no rights – they belonged to their owners and were not treated as human beings. In the late 18th century slave owners were worried that it might become harder to get new slaves from Africa. They encouraged slaves to marry and have children. But often they would sell members of a family to different owners. Olaudah Equiano wrote about a slave sale in Barbados in the late 18th century: '... there were several

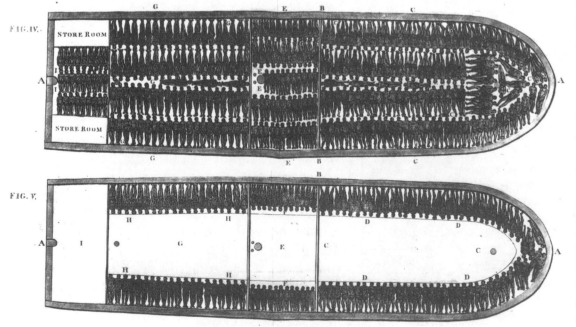

Slave Children

The child of a slave mother was also a slave. Children started work as young as four years old, doing simple jobs like weeding. Older children looked after the younger ones while their mother was working. Between about 10 and 14, children took on the same work as adults.

brothers who, in the sale, were sold in different lots; and it was very moving on this occasion to see and hear their cries at parting.'

Rules and Punishment

Slave owners tried to control their slaves with harsh rules. Slaves had to do whatever work they were told to do. They could not leave the plantation without permission and were not allowed to own property. On most Caribbean islands, slaves were not allowed to learn to read and write. Slaves who broke the rules were whipped. They might have an ear or even a hand cut off. In the worst cases they were killed.

The Profits from Slavery

Like the plantation owners, the European countries involved in the slave trade became rich. From the 18th century Britain prospered from the slave trade. New industries grew up to process the goods, such as sugar cane, from the colonies. Bristol and Liverpool became big ports where slave ships were prepared. The wealth from the slave trade helped Britain to become the first country to undergo an industrial revolution.

The End of the Slave Trade

Slave workers on the Caribbean island of Antigua.

By the end of the 18th century many people were protesting against slavery. There were slave rebellions and anti-slavery campaigns in Britain and the USA.

Stopping the Slave Trade in Britain

In the late 18th century certain religious groups, such as the Methodists and Quakers, were against slavery. Some white working people, who were fighting for more rights for themselves, supported rights for black slaves. Black people such as Ottobah Cuguano, Olaudah Equiano, and Mary Prince were involved in the campaign. In her book of 1831 Mary Prince wrote 'Liberty. That is what we want. We do not mind hard work, if we had proper treatment, and proper wages.'

The anti-slavery campaign in Parliament was led by William Wilberforce. In 1807 the British slave trade was stopped, but it was not until 1833 that all slaves were finally freed.

Ending Slavery in the USA

In 1833 the American Anti-Slavery Society was set up. It included black campaigners such as Sojourner Truth and Frederick Douglass. Harriet Tubman, an escaped slave herself, helped about 300 slaves to escape to Canada in the 1850s. However, slaves were not freed until after the American Civil War of 1861 to 1865. During the war the Northern states, led by President Abraham Lincoln, fought to free the slaves. The Southern states, where most of the slave owners lived, were keen to keep slavery. Black people formed one-tenth of the Union (Northern) Army. In 1865 slavery finally became illegal throughout the USA.

Nat Turner's Rebellion

The biggest rebellion in the USA was led by Nat Turner in Virginia in 1831. Turner and about 70 other slaves killed slave owners and freed their slaves. After about two months he and 55 other rebels were caught and hanged. White gangs then murdered about 200 other slaves to punish black people for the rebellion.

Sojourner Truth.

Sojourner Truth (about 1797–1883)

Sojourner Truth, whose legal name was Isabella Baumtree, was born a slave. She was badly treated by her owners as a child. Between 1810 and 1827 she had at least five children with another slave. In 1827 she ran away and a couple of years later went to New York City with her two youngest children.

In 1843 she felt that God had told her to preach. She left New York, taking the name Sojourner Truth, and travelled around the country to campaign against slavery. During the 1850s she started to speak out for women's rights too. When the Civil War started Truth gathered supplies for the black soldiers. Then, in 1864, she went to Washington, DC, where she helped black people from the South to find jobs and homes, and met President Abraham Lincoln. In 1875 Truth returned to Michigan and stayed there until she died.

Toussaint-L'Ouverture (about 1743–1803)

There were many slave rebellions in the Caribbean. Led by Toussaint-L'Ouverture, the slaves of French St Dominique freed their island from white rule. By 1800 Toussaint-L'Ouverture controlled St Dominique. But in 1801 the new French ruler, Napoleon Bonaparte, sent an army there to conquer it again and bring back slavery. The French were beaten in the end, but Toussaint-L'Ouverture himself was captured by the French and taken to France, where he died in 1803. He told Napoleon 'By overthrowing me, you have only cut down the trunk of the tree of liberty of St Dominique. Its roots will grow back, for they are many and deep.' In 1804 the people of St Dominique formed an independent state called Haiti, the first independent nation in Latin America.

Francois Dominique Toussaint-L'Ouverture.

The Wild West

A settler wagon train crossing the Great Plains with the Rocky Mountains in the background.

When the USA first became an independent country at the end of the 18th century, it was made up of just 13 small states on the east coast of North America. But the new nation was ambitious. By 1850 it had bought or won land in war right across the continent, from the Atlantic Ocean to the Pacific.

Mountain Men

In 1803 the USA doubled in size when it bought the huge territory of Louisiana from France. Soon, Americans began to explore the lands west of the Mississippi River. Among the first people to move west were fur trappers. There were plenty of beavers in the forests of the Rocky Mountains, and in the early 19th century their furs were valuable. The trappers, or 'mountain men', often travelling alone, explored the best routes across the empty plains and rugged mountains of the west.

Settlers and Miners

Once the mountain men had opened up trails to the west coast, settlers (people who wanted to settle in a new place) followed. Unlike the mountain men, the settlers did not travel light. They brought along all their belongings in covered wagons, pulled by oxen. These lumbering wagons had to travel along difficult trails designed only for horses and pack mules.

At first, most settlers headed for Oregon. But in 1848 gold was discovered in California, and thousands of fortune-hunters headed there the following year. By 1852 California had over 15 times more people than it had in 1848.

The Railways Arrive

By the 1850s there were many railways in the eastern USA, and a few railways in the west. During the 1860s plans were laid for new railway routes across the continent. The first, from Omaha, in Nebraska, to Sacramento, in

The Native Americans

When the first white explorers arrived in the Great Plains they found Native Americans already living there. The Native Americans hunted buffalo for food and clothing, following the buffalo herds from place to place. Soon white settlers began to clash with the Native Americans. The US government tried to keep the peace by agreeing that the Native Americans could live undisturbed in some areas if they let whites settle in other areas. But white miners or farmers broke each agreement almost as soon as it was signed. During the 1850s and 1860s the Cheyenne and Sioux made war on the settlers. The US army was called in, and thousands of Native Americans were killed. White hunters also killed the vast buffalo herds, destroying the Native Americans' way of life. By the end of the century, the settlers had 'won the west' from the Native Americans, who were left with nothing.

Sitting Bull, a great leader of the Sioux group of Native American tribes.

California, was opened in 1869. The journey time by stagecoach had been over 21 days. By rail, the trip took just one week.

In Texas, far to the south of the first railway line, huge herds of cattle roamed the prairies. With the coming of the railways, Texan cattle ranchers realized that they could get more money for their cows by selling them to provide food for big cities in the east. Once each year, the cattlemen sent herds of cows hundreds of miles north across the Great Plains to markets at railway towns.

The people who looked after the cattle on the long, difficult trail to market were cowboys. When they were not rounding up cattle or branding them, the cowboys were 'breaking' wild horses for riding. On the trail, they could expect blistering heat, dust, terrible storms, and

A cowboy takes aim at a Native American.

hostile Native Americans. Worst of all was the danger of the herd stampeding.

The End of the West

By the 1890s the frontier between west and east had gone. The western territories were now states, with their own governments, towns, and cities. The west was no longer 'wild'.

The American Civil War

The Causes of the War

Since the early 17th century there had been large cotton-growing farms known as plantations in the southern states of the USA. The big landowners used black slaves from Africa to work on their plantations. In the northern states there was more industry and the farms were smaller, and slaves were not used. These states were against slavery, and this resulted in great arguments between the pro-slavery and anti-slavery states in the US Congress (parliament). In 1860 the Americans elected a new president, Abraham Lincoln, who was opposed to slavery.

Eleven southern states refused to accept Lincoln as president. They decided to elect their own president. They formed themselves into the Confederacy, and left the Union. Lincoln wanted the states to remain united, but it was impossible as the two sides could not agree, and in 1861 war broke out.

Abraham Lincoln, who some think was the greatest of all America's presidents.

Union state

slave state that stayed in the Union

Confederate state

North and South at War

Most of the fighting in the first two years of the war was in the state of Virginia. Here the Confederate (southern) forces – commanded by Robert E Lee and Thomas 'Stonewall' Jackson – concentrated on defending their capital, Richmond. These two generals and their armies either held or defeated the Union (northern) armies at Bull Run, the Seven Days' Battle, Antietam, Chancellorsville, and Fredericksburg. But the North could always replace its heavy losses in men and equipment whereas the South

Battle of the Ironclads

The American Civil War was notable for an experiment with armour-plated warships or 'ironclads'. On 9 March 1862 two odd-looking ships, the Confederate *Merrimac* and the Union *Monitor,* fought each other off the coast of Virginia. The cannonballs of both ships bounced off each other's armour and the battle ended in stalemate.

Robert E Lee (1807–1870)

Robert E Lee was the most famous of all the Civil War generals. He won many victories against larger enemy armies and was worshipped by his troops. Although he was a Southerner, he was actually offered the command of the Union armies once war had broken out. Lee refused, preferring to be loyal to his home state of Virginia, even though he believed that the splitting of the Union was wrong.

A Confederate encampment near Atlanta, Georgia.

Union troops from a New York regiment.

fought on. Although southern generals continued to inflict heavy losses on Grant's armies at Chattanooga, the Wilderness, and Cold Harbor, all the time Lee's forces grew weaker.

Further to the south the two Union generals Philip Sheridan and William Tecumseh Sherman did terrible damage to the Shenandoah Valley and Georgia respectively, and this forced the Confederates to abandon Richmond, their capital, in the state of Virginia. Lee's position became hopeless and on 9 April 1865 he surrendered to Grant, so ending the Civil War.

could not, mainly because the Union navy stopped vital supplies from reaching the South. The South had little of its own industry, and had to import most of what it needed to fight the war.

In the west the Union general Ulysses Grant won many successes which forced Lee to act differently. Lee invaded the north and threatened the capital, Washington. A Union army met Lee at Gettysburg and after a three-day battle Lee was forced to retreat. His losses were impossible to replace, but the South

The Aftermath

The South was ruined. The war had cost the lives of over 600,000 men. Lincoln was assassinated by John Wilkes Booth before he could begin to repair the divisions caused by the war, and there was great bitterness in the South for many years.

The Age of Empire: The British in India

British territory in 1858

The British East India Company

The East India Company was set up in 1600 by Queen Elizabeth I to look after the interests of British traders who were trading in silks and cottons with the Moguls (rulers of India from 1526 onwards). The Company was made up of a number of traders who helped each other. By

the mid-18th century they had set up their own army. This army defeated the French, the Company's main rival in India, and the British became the most powerful force in India.

As the power of the Mogul empire declined, so the territory of the Company grew as it took over more and more Indian states in a process they called 'annexation'. The Company took over the Mogul system of taxing even the poorest people on their crops and income. They not only traded in goods but also in people. Since slavery had been abolished, a new system called 'indentured labour' was introduced. Indian people were taken from their land and sent to work for five years on sugar plantations in the West Indies. They often did not come back. That is why many of the people in the Caribbean today are of Indian origin.

Lakshmibai, Rani of Jhansi (1835–1858)

The Rani of Jhansi became a heroine of the Indian Mutiny. Her husband, the Rajah (king) of Jhansi, had died in 1853, and because she had no son to become rajah, the East India Company had taken his land. She wanted to cooperate with the British government and asked them for help. When they refused she began to hate them. She led the rebels in the Mutiny, fighting with them in Jhansi and Gwalior. She died at the age of 22 defending the fort at Gwalior. She is still a symbol of female bravery.

The Rani of Jhansi.

The Great Indian Peninsular Terminus – part of the massive amount of railway building that was carried out in India.

The Indian Mutiny, 1857–1858

In 1857 many Indian sepoys (soldiers serving the East India Company) rebelled against the British. They were angry about the British annexation of Oudh and about the cartridges they had been given for their guns. Rumours spread that these had been greased with the fat of pigs or cows. Before loading them the soldiers had to bite off their ends. Muslims will not touch pig meat and the cow is sacred to Hindus. For any of them to bite off the end of such a cartridge would be a sin.

Fighting quickly spread all over the north of India and the mutiny turned into a more general revolt against British rule and the introduction of Western ways in India. British people were trapped and forced to surrender in several cities, and many British and Indian people were killed, including innocent children.

After the Mutiny, the British brutally punished the rebels. Any Indian who was captured after the revolt (even if they had not been part of the Mutiny) could be hanged, and many were blown from cannons to teach the others a lesson.

Back in Britain the government was so alarmed at this rebellion that they decided to take the government of India into their own hands. The East India Company was abandoned, India became a British colony, and Queen Victoria became Empress of India.

The Effects of Colonialism

By 1857 the British had built 320 kilometres (200 miles) of railway in India. After the Mutiny railways were built in earnest because the British had found communications so difficult during the Mutiny. By 1905 there were 45,060 kilometres (28,000 miles) of track in India. This not only helped in transporting soldiers to trouble spots but also in transporting goods to the coast for export. The Indian railway system is still one of the most extensive in the world.

Trade with India made many British people rich, but did nothing to help the majority of the Indian population, who were very poor. The taxes which the British Raj (government in India) continued to take made the people even poorer.

The Scramble for Africa

Africa in 1880

In 1880 most of Africa was still ruled by Africans. Only a few Europeans lived in the continent. Most lived in trading posts on the coast, although some missionaries had travelled further into the interior. The slave trade was over, and West Africans had benefited from the education brought by the missionaries. Some of them had become so rich through trade in crops that they sent their children to university in Europe. The Scottish missionary explorer David Livingstone had brought churches and schools to East Africa.

The only part of black Africa where Europeans lived in greater numbers was South Africa, where many British and Boers (Dutch settlers) had come. During the 19th century many Boers had migrated northwards, setting up their own republics and coming into conflict with the powerful Zulu people. The British were already fighting the Boers over the new lands, which were rich in gold and diamonds.

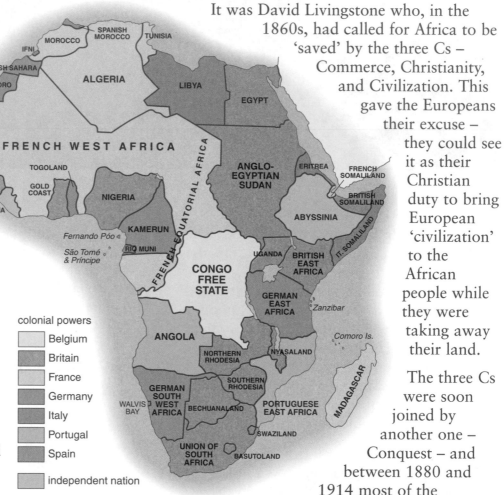

colonial powers

- Belgium
- Britain
- France
- Germany
- Italy
- Portugal
- Spain

- independent nation

Europe in the 1880s

The spread of industrialization in Europe meant that European countries were in competition with each other to control the sources of raw materials, such as cotton, coffee, tea, and palm oil, for their factories. They were also looking for new customers for the goods they produced in the factories. Many African leaders were happy with their relationship with Europe in 1880 and the benefits that European education

and trade had brought. They believed that their warriors were strong enough to stop the Europeans taking control of their land. What the Africans did not know was that the Europeans now had new guns, including the rapid-fire Maxim and Gatling guns – forerunners of modern machine-guns. African armies only had spears, bows and arrows, and old-fashioned guns.

The Three Cs

It was David Livingstone who, in the 1860s, had called for Africa to be 'saved' by the three Cs – Commerce, Christianity, and Civilization. This gave the Europeans their excuse – they could see it as their Christian duty to bring European 'civilization' to the African people while they were taking away their land.

The three Cs were soon joined by another one – Conquest – and between 1880 and 1914 most of the continent came under the control of seven European countries. Many battles were fought, many Africans died, and many starved because their crops had been burnt.

After the conquest the Europeans' biggest problem was to get the people to work for them. The British did this in some places by introducing a hut tax. The only way Africans could get the money to pay this tax on their homes was to work for the Europeans. In the

Cecil Rhodes is shown striding across the African continent.

The Zulu chief Sirayo.

Belgian Congo, people who refused to carry rubber to the coast for export were either shot or had their hands chopped off.

Rulers who Disobeyed

King Prempeh, the Ashanti (or Asante) ruler in the Gold Coast, refused British offers of help to keep the French from taking his land. He was captured in the Ashanti War of 1896 and exiled to the Seychelles (islands in the Indian Ocean) until 1925.

In South Africa, Cetshwayo, King of the Zulus, welcomed the British taking the Transvaal (a diamond-rich area) and promised to protect them from the Boers. He was later to be captured at the Battle of Ulundi in 1879 and imprisoned in Cape Town until 1883. He died in battle in 1884.

In Matabeleland (now in Zimbabwe) the Ndbele chief Lobengula was tricked into giving his land to Cecil Rhodes for mining. Misunderstandings led to war and Lobengula committed suicide rather than be captured by the white people.

The Age of Empire: Australia and New Zealand

The Aborigines in Australia

The Aborigines, meaning 'inhabitants from earliest times', were the original Australians and are thought to have come from southeast Asia over 40,000 years ago. They lived in Australia as hunters and gatherers, fishing and hunting for fish and meat, and gathering fruit and vegetables. For a long time, rough seas prevented explorers from landing in Australia and the Aborigines were the only people living there.

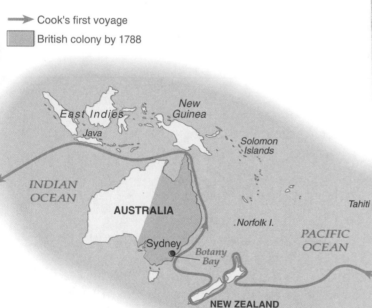

Cook's first voyage
British colony by 1788

An Australian Aboriginal bark painting showing a funeral ceremony.

New Zealand and the Maoris

The Maoris came originally from Polynesia and had lived in New Zealand since around AD 750. They called the country Aotearoa, meaning 'Land of the Long White Cloud'. Captain James Cook visited New Zealand in 1769 and he was followed by European whalers, traders, and missionaries. British settlers began to arrive in the early 19th century. At this time there were about 250,000 Maoris in New Zealand. Around a quarter of the Maori population was killed in wars with the settlers, and, as in Australia, the diseases brought by the settlers killed many more. Weakened by fighting, the Maoris accepted British rule in exchange for a British promise in the Treaty of Waitangi (1840) to let them keep their land.

Almost immediately British greed for more land led to wars that lasted until 1870. Maori land was bought for a very low price by the government and given to British settlers. The British settlers brought some benefit to the Maoris – new crops such as wheat, potatoes, and apples were traded with the Europeans – and schools were built, bringing literacy. Many Maoris, however, felt that the advantages were outweighed by the loss of their independence, culture, and civilization.

New Zealand had its own gold rush in 1860, and the settlers exported wool and gold to Britain. Later, when refrigeration improved, they exported lamb, mutton, and butter.

Early European Settlement

In 1770 British Captain James Cook sailed into Botany Bay (near modern Sydney) and claimed the whole of the east coast of Australia for Britain, naming it New South Wales. He took scientists and artists with him who studied the unique plants and animals, and observed the peoples. They greatly added to scientific knowledge and increased European interest in Australia.

Convicted criminals from Britain were among the first people to settle in Australia. They were sent there because the jails in England were too full. In 1787 Captain Arthur Philip sailed from Britain with over 750 convicts and set up a penal colony (a place where convicted criminals were sent) at Port Jackson. Some convicts were shipped there with their families, and many men, women, and children died on the long voyage.

As convict settlements moved inland, the Europeans infected Aborigine communities with their diseases. A smallpox epidemic in 1789 killed half the Aborigines living between Botany Bay and Broken Bay. More settlements were made at Hobart, Newcastle, Norfolk Island, and Brisbane. Explorers and free settlers followed the convicts, and cities such as Perth, Melbourne, and Adelaide grew up. In the 19th century most of the Aboriginal tribes around the coast and in eastern Australia were killed in violent battles with white settlers. In Tasmania almost the whole Aboriginal population was massacred. Settlers took Aborigine land. In return for slave labour on the farms they let the Aborigines visit the sacred places that were important to their religion.

Banksia – one of the previously unknown plants discovered in Australia.

At first the settlers had to import food from Britain, and they paid for this in sealskins, seal oil, and sandalwood. Many of them later became farmers and exported wool and wheat to Europe. After the 1880s frozen meat was exported.

A tramway in Tasmania operated by convict power!

The Discovery of Gold

Gold was discovered in Australia in the 1850s. This gave the economy the boost it needed and helped the cities to grow by attracting more people and business. Railways were built to transport gold and other minerals to the coast. There were two gold 'rushes', one in the 1850s and one in the 1880s. People went further and further inland searching for the gold that would make them rich.

Punishment and Poverty in Ireland

By the 18th century Ireland had been under English rule for 600 years. The Irish had tried many times to drive out the English, but without success. English people owned most of the land, and most Irish people were poor and badly treated. Religious differences were another source of conflict. The Irish were Catholics and the English were Protestants.

The Penal Code

The English set up an Irish government, which was also Protestant. The English and Irish governments passed a series of anti-Catholic laws from 1695 to 1727. These laws were called the Penal Code, and they declared that anybody who did not follow the Protestant Anglican religion could not attend school or work in government, the law, or most other professions. Catholics could not vote in elections either. These laws left the Irish with no power or influence in their own country. A minority of the population in Ireland followed the Presbyterian faith, a different form of Protestant religion, and the laws were also against them.

Although there were some educated, middle-class Irish people, the majority of the Irish lived as peasant farmers on land owned by rich English landlords. These peasants suffered terrible hardship because they had to pay high rents to their landlords. If an Irish person

Catholics and Protestants

Even after many Penal Code laws were abolished, Protestants still held the power in Ireland. The largest population of Protestants was in the northern province of Ulster. They were constantly worried that the Catholics might one day take back their land and property. In the late 18th century Protestant groups were formed that persecuted Catholics in Ulster, turning them out of their homes and sometimes murdering them. Catholics then formed groups to protect themselves and battles took place constantly between the groups.

The Revolution of 1798

Wolfe Tone, founder of the Society of United Irishmen, who fought for Irish independence.

In 1789 the French Revolution broke out and the king of France and his government were overthrown. News of the revolution spread across Europe. Governments were alarmed, but people with revolutionary ideas felt optimistic that change could really happen. In 1791 an Irish Presbyterian lawyer called Wolfe Tone founded the Society of United Irishmen. This political party was based on French revolutionary ideas. Wolfe Tone appealed both to Protestants and Catholics to unite and establish an Irish government free from English rule.

In 1794 the English government banned revolutionary parties like the United Irishmen and sent in troops to capture their members. Any people suspected of treason were arrested, tortured by often very nasty methods, and sometimes shot. In 1798 a major Irish uprising took place, but was quickly crushed. Wolfe Tone was arrested and put in prison, where he committed suicide.

Irish rebels attack the home of an English officer during the uprising of 1798.

refused an order made by his English landlord, he or she would be punished, possibly by being beaten. Since these poor farmers were treated little better than slaves, and the English grew very rich from their hard work, Irish resentment of the English was intense.

As the 18th century progressed, some politicians in Ireland began to be more sympathetic towards the Catholics. In 1793 the government abolished many of the Penal Code laws and allowed Catholics to vote in elections. However, the Catholics were still forbidden to hold posts in government.

An Irish rebellion that took place in 1798 was quickly crushed. The English government decided they could control Ireland better themselves. In 1801 they abolished the Irish parliament and the Act of Union between England and Ireland came into force.

Lives of the Poor

Most Irish farmers and their children lived in dingy cabins that had only one room. These cabins had walls made of mud mixed with straw and had no windows. Families and their farm animals would sleep on straw spread across the floor. Meals consisted mostly of potatoes, which were cheap and easy to grow, but families were often hungry and had to beg for food. These terrible conditions led to thousands moving to North America in search of a better life.

The English ruling class lived in homes such as this, while ordinary Irish people lived in poverty.

Conflict and Famine in Ireland

In the 18th century the Industrial Revolution began in Britain. Powerful machines were developed, which meant that people could no longer work in their homes but had to work where the machines were, in factories. The part of Ireland that benefited from this revolution was the northeast of Ulster. Old industries expanded and new ones, such as shipbuilding, flourished.

Both Catholics and Protestants flocked to Belfast city, the centre of Ulster's industry, to get work. Protestants in Ulster felt that their new-found prosperity depended on Ireland's continued union with Britain.

The Catholic Association

The 1801 Act of Union had created the United Kingdom of Great Britain and Ireland. However, Irish Catholics had no political power in this union. In 1823 a new Irish organization called the Catholic Association was created. Led by a lawyer named Daniel O'Connell, it called for full rights for Catholics.

O'Connell constantly pressurized the British government and led peaceful protests. He became extremely popular amongst Irish Catholics. In 1829, fearing a major uprising, the government passed the Catholic Emancipation Act. It granted new rights to Catholics, including the right to sit in Parliament and be a member of the government. In the same year O'Connell was elected as a member of the British Parliament.

The Fenian Society

A movement called the Fenian Society was founded in 1858. The Fenians believed that Ireland could only be freed from British rule by force. They planned to attack military targets both in Ireland and England. Many Fenians were caught, imprisoned, and executed. They failed to make Ireland independent, but they made British politicians realize political changes were needed in Ireland.

The Irish Famine

The ordinary people of Ireland were among the poorest in Europe. Most Irish people ate little but potatoes. When the potato crops of 1845 and 1846 were ruined by disease, millions found themselves without food. Rich landlords continued to export grain and other food products from Ireland while the British government sent little help. Across Ireland starving people raked the land searching for potatoes. Dead, unburied bodies lay in fields and by the road. As a result, the population fell by around 2 million within four years. About a million people died and a further million emigrated, mainly to the USA.

The Irish Home Rule Party

In 1870 the Home Government Association party was created. It wanted Ireland to have its own government with the power to make decisions about its own affairs. Charles Stewart Parnell became leader of the party in 1878. A brilliant leader, he managed to make British politicians pay attention to Ireland's problems. However, despite the efforts of the British prime minister, William Gladstone, to establish Irish home rule, other politicians blocked it.

The Revival of Irish Culture

The English had tried to stamp out Irish culture. However, in the late 19th century a revival took place. People began to play Irish sports again. A society led by Douglas Hyde promoted Irish literature, language, and poetry. A young poet called William Butler Yeats was writing verse based on Irish myths and legends. Another writer, John Millington Synge, wrote plays portraying ordinary Irish people. However, not all Irish audiences liked the way they were portrayed. One of Synge's plays, performed in a Dublin theatre, caused a riot.

Daniel O'Connell (1775–1847)

Born to a middle-class Catholic family in 1775, Daniel O'Connell was educated in France because there were no schools for Catholic children in Ireland then. He became a lawyer in 1798. He was the first Irish Catholic in the British Parliament. In Ireland he is known as 'the Liberator' because he won rights for Catholics.

William Butler Yeats (1865–1939)

The poet William Butler Yeats was born in 1865 in Dublin, the son of an Irish painter. He learned to love Irish tradition from his childhood holidays in Sligo in the west of Ireland. He particularly loved Irish myths and legends and the supernatural and was a leader in the 'Celtic revival'. He is one of the most brilliant and famous of Irish writers.

Charles Stewart Parnell, leader of the Home Rule (formerly Home Government) Association.

Starving people try to steal food from a potato store.

South America Frees Itself

Napoleon and Freedom

After Columbus's discovery of the 'New World' in 1492, Spain and Portugal divided the whole of South America between themselves. The Native Americans who lived there were treated cruelly, forced to work as slaves. They had not been able to break free. But after 1807 the French emperor Napoleon took over Spain and Portugal. This gave the Spanish and Portuguese too much to do at home to have time to look after their colonies.

Confusion in Europe gave the South American people a chance to fight for the independence they had dreamed of. Over the next two decades nearly all the Spanish and Portuguese colonies in the Americas won their freedom. The main wars of liberation involved two major nationalist forces. One was led by the Venezuelans Simón Bolívar and Antonio José de Sucre, and the other, the Army of the Andes, was led by José de San Martin of Argentina and Bernardo O'Higgins from Chile.

During the 19th century some South American countries were at war with each other. This picture shows Paraguay capturing the town of Paysandu in Uruguay in 1865.

Simón Bolívar (1783–1830)

Simón Bolívar, known as 'the Liberator', is now the national hero of Venezuela, Colombia, Ecuador, Peru, and Bolivia, although he was hated at the time of his death. He was born in Caracas, Venezuela, in 1783 and travelled in Europe before returning to play an important part in the wars of liberation. In 1819 he was chosen as president of Gran Colombia (now Colombia, Venezuela, Panama, and Ecuador). He then took charge of the last campaigns of independence in Peru and defeated the Spanish in 1824. He created the new state of Bolivia in 1825. He was the most powerful man on the continent but his vision of a united South America was not to be. In 1826 he returned to the north to find political disagreement. The people did not like him making all the decisions without listening to anyone else. By 1830 he had had enough and resigned. He died in the same year.

Freedom – But Who Owns the Land?

The population of South America is a mixture of Native American people, black descendants of African slaves, a minority of white people, and mestizos (people of mixed race).

Before the wars of independence there was a division between the masses of ordinary people and the few rich people. The rich people owned

After independence European and American people settled in the new countries. Companies invested money, and mining companies, fruit plantations, and oil refineries were set up. The *hacienda* system suited the Europeans and Americans. It meant that they did not have to pay much for the raw materials. They could export these materials to their own countries and make a lot of money. In the late 19th

Farmers threshing corn in Chile.

most of the land and ran the government. After independence not much changed. The huge farms (*haciendas*) were still owned and run by a few powerful families. All the hard work was done by the poor peasants for little money while the landlords took the profits. Some peasants had a little land of their own and some had none. The poorest people were the descendants of black slaves. Countries were run by *caudillos*, who had been the military war leaders. They ran the countries using the same principles as were used when operating the *haciendas*. This meant that society was still organized along racial lines with the white people at the top and the black ex-slaves at the bottom.

century many people emigrated from Europe to South America, and a lot of European money was invested. Railways were built and ocean transport improved. All these factors helped make the countries of South America richer.

The unequal ownership of land still exists in South American countries today, although some governments have tried to introduce land reforms to improve life for the poor people. However, in many places poor farmers have been forced to leave their family farms to make way for commercial farms run by multinational companies.

Europeans Exploring Africa

Europeans were fascinated by Africa – it seemed an exotic and mysterious place to them. In the 19th century hardly a year went by when an exploratory expedition was not sent. The explorers were looking for different things – the sources of rivers, ancient cities, mountains, exotic plants, and animals. Some explorers wanted to write books about their travels and others to paint the beautiful flowers, birds, and butterflies. Missionaries went to take the word of their God to people they saw as uncivilized, and traders went to find raw materials for European factories.

Famous European Explorers

Frenchman René Caillié led an expedition to Timbuktu (now in Mali) in the 1820s, and German missionaries Ludwig Krapf and Johannes Rebman were the first Europeans to see Mount Kilimanjaro, the highest mountain in Africa, in 1848. Pierre de Brazza was a French explorer who founded the country that is now the Congo. The most famous British explorers of the 19th century were John Speke, Richard Burton, David Livingstone, and Henry Morton

Stanley. Several women explorers travelled alone in Africa, including Mary Kingsley, who studied African religion and law and wrote *Travels in West Africa* (1897), and Marianne North, a painter of plants who travelled in southern Africa. Her paintings are collected in Kew Gardens, London.

The Source of the River Nile

In 1857 John Hanning Speke and Richard Burton were sent by the British Royal Geographical Society to find the source of the White Nile. They travelled from the island of Zanzibar with 132 African porters and 36 mules to Lake Tanganyika. Speke and Burton always argued ferociously about where the source was. Speke correctly recognized the lake he had called Lake Victoria after his queen as the source. However Burton disagreed, and there was to be a public debate between them in London in September 1864.

Speke died the day before this meeting. Burton wrote: 'The charitable say that he shot himself, the uncharitable say that I shot him'. The coroner at the time said Speke's death was an accident.

'Dr Livingstone, I Presume'

These famous words were uttered by the journalist Henry Morton Stanley, a Welshman working for the *New York Herald,* who mounted a huge expedition with 200 porters and numerous camels and donkeys to find David Livingstone. Livingstone was a missionary who had travelled to Africa to settle the dispute about the source of the Nile, and nobody in Britain had heard from him for four years. Stanley

Legend:
—— Burton and Speke 1857–1859
—— David Livingstone 1841–1856
----- David Livingstone and Henry Stanley 1866–1873
—— Henry Stanley 1871–1872 and 1874–1877

This map shows the routes of some of the great African explorations.

David Livingstone (1813–1873)

David Livingstone was born in Blantyre, Scotland, and spent his youth working in a cotton mill. After he finished his education he became a missionary doctor. He first arrived in Cape Town in 1841 and explored much of southern and eastern Africa for the next 28 years, spreading Christianity. In 1844 he was seriously mauled by a lion and lost the use of his left arm. His most famous discovery was Victoria Falls, in what is now Zimbabwe. He campaigned against the slave trade, and in 1866 he went to seek the source of the Nile to settle the disagreement between Burton and Speke. After his meeting with Stanley he began his last journey but fell ill with dysentery and died. His devoted servants travelled for nine months to the coast with his embalmed body. He was buried in Westminster Abbey, London, in April 1874.

found Livingstone in the village of Ujiji, near Lake Tanganyika – he was very ill but refused to come home. Stanley continued his explorations after this meeting and became very rich.

These explorers wrote a lot about the people they met on their journeys, but few Africans wrote what they thought about the Europeans. We know that most of the explorers were surrounded by Africans who were loyal to them. In the 1950s and 1960s African novelists such as Chinua Achebe and Ngugi wa Thiong'o began writing about the Africans' first encounters with the strange-looking people who were to change their lives.

The very ill David Livingstone is helped into his hut at the end of his last journey.

The Unification of Italy and Germany

Lands under the control of the

Kingdom of Sardinia

Pope

Spanish Bourbon family

Austrian empire

At the beginning of the 19th century Italy and Germany were made up of many different states. The rulers of the states were content to leave things as they were, but many people wanted unification. Unification would bring all the states together to form one Italy and one Germany.

Italy

After Napoleon's defeat in 1815, the northwestern state of Sardinia-Piedmont was the only Italian state ruled by Italians. Every other Italian state was ruled by a foreign power. The north and northeast of Italy were part of the Austrian empire. Those in the south were ruled by the Spanish Bourbon family, which also ruled Spain. In the centre of the country, the pope ruled Rome, the Papal States, and other neighbouring states.

The prime minister of Sardinia-Piedmont, Count Camillo di Cavour, was a nationalist who believed that all of Italy should be controlled by Italians. With the help of France, he drove Austria out of Italy in 1859 and the following year his armies took over the Papal States.

In the same year, the Italian revolutionary Giuseppe Garibaldi gained control of Sicily and Naples (the Two Sicilies) in the south, and in 1861 Victor Emmanuel II of Sardinia-Piedmont was crowned king of Italy.

Giuseppe Garibaldi (1807–1882)

Giuseppe Garibaldi was an Italian soldier whose lifelong wish was to see a united Italy free from foreign rule. He was a revolutionary from a young age, and many times he was forced into exile or threatened with death. He always managed to escape, and his courage and determination never to surrender made him a popular hero. In 1860, with his army of about 1,000 soldiers (called Redshirts because of their uniform), he landed in Sicily and proclaimed himself dictator. He defeated the army of the king of Naples and captured first Palermo then Naples. To achieve his dream of unification, Garibaldi handed all of southern Italy over to Victor Emmanuel II, King of Sardinia-Piedmont, in 1860. Victor Emmanuel became king of Italy in the following year.

Garibaldi's fame spread throughout the world. Abraham Lincoln, President of the USA, asked him to command the Federal troops in the American Civil War, and in 1864 he was cheered through the streets of England.

Timeline: Unification of Italy (1859–1870)

1859	Sardinia-Piedmont takes control of Lombardy.
1860	Sardinia-Piedmont takes control of Tuscany, Modena, and Parma.
1860	Garibaldi takes control of Sicily and Naples and hands them over to Victor Emmanuel II.
1860	The Papal States become part of Italy.
1861	Victor Emmanuel II becomes king of a unified Italy.
1866	Venice becomes part of Italy.
1870	Rome becomes part of Italy.

Garibaldi meets King Victor Emmanuel in October 1860.

Germany

After Napoleon defeated the Holy Roman Empire in 1806 the 39 German states were formed into the German Confederation. The confederation contained the small German states and the larger and more powerful country of Austria. The confederation was dominated by Austria, which did not want German unification. In 1862 Otto von Bismarck became prime minister of Prussia, one of the German states. He believed that Prussia could only become a first-rate power if Germany were unified. In 1866 he took the first step towards this goal by defeating Austria in the Seven Weeks' War. Seventeen small German

Otto von Bismarck (1815–1898)

Otto von Bismarck was a Prussian politician who founded the German Empire and was its first chancellor. As a young man he disapproved of the 1848 revolutions and supported the king. In 1862 he became prime minister of Prussia, the most powerful of the German states. He determined to establish Prussia as the leader of a united Germany, and in the 1860s he waged aggressive wars against Denmark, Austria, and France to achieve his aim. Known as the 'Iron Chancellor', Bismarck continued to hold power in the united Germany until 1890.

Timeline: Unification of Germany (1861–1871)

1861	William I becomes king of Prussia.
1862	Bismarck is appointed Prussia's prime minister.
1864	The Danish territory of Schleswig-Holstein becomes part of the German Confederation after a short war.
1866	Prussia defeats Austria, and the North German Confederation is set up.
1871	Prussia wins the Franco-Prussian War and takes Alsace and Lorraine.
1871	The German Empire is established.

States, united to form the North German Confederation, which excluded Austria. France tried to stop Prussia's growing power, but in 1871 France was defeated and Germany took the eastern provinces of Alsace and Lorraine from France. The governments of the southern German states joined with the North German Confederation to form a united German nation called the German Empire. By the early 20th century the unified Germany had become Europe's leading industrial nation.

Russia under the Tsars

The title 'tsar' (meaning emperor) of Russia was first adopted in 1547 by Ivan the Terrible. The word tsar comes from the Latin *caesar* – the title used by the rulers of ancient Rome. The tsars had total control of Russia. Under their rule Russia expanded from a collection of small states in eastern Europe to an empire that stretched across Asia to the Pacific Ocean.

Catherine II, known as Catheriine the Great.

Russia Grows in Power

When Peter the Great (ruled 1682–1725) became tsar, Russia was a backward, unimportant country compared to the great powers in Europe. To transform Russia, Peter introduced modern European ways. He entered into a series of wars in Europe that turned Russia into a major European power. In one of these wars he took land on the eastern shore of the Baltic Sea from Sweden, so beginning Russia's westward expansion into Europe.

Catherine the Great (ruled 1762–1796) continued Russia's expansion, conquering the Crimea on the Black Sea and much of Poland. Catherine loved European art and culture and encouraged the building of schools and roads. Early in her reign she planned to help the serfs – peasants who were like slaves and were owned by rich landlords. However, the French

Serfdom

A rich landowner had complete control over his serfs' lives. They had to get his permission to marry and were not allowed to leave their owner's property. Serfs could be bought, sold, or punished according to their master's wishes. During the Crimean War (1853–1856) Tsar Nicholas I forced thousands of serfs to fight. With no war experience, freezing weather, and little food, serfs died in large numbers. Most landowners cared little for their serfs, sometimes even using serfs as betting stakes when gambling. Serfdom was abolished in 1861, but most of the freed serfs found that they were no better off.

A village fair in the Ukraine.

Russian workers repairing a railway line.

Alexander III (ruled 1881–1894)

Having seen his father assassinated, Alexander III decided to rule harshly. He persecuted any groups he saw as enemies, such as secret societies. He was particularly hard on Jewish people. He only allowed them to live in certain areas and restricted what jobs they could do. Alexander and his government spread false rumours about Jews to Christian Russians, which encouraged hatred. Christian mobs carried out frequent attacks on Jews. These attacks were called pogroms (Russian for 'devastation'), and on one occasion mobs in over 200 cities and towns attacked Jews and destroyed their property.

Leo Tolstoy (1828–1910)

The novelist Leo Tolstoy was the son of a rich landowner. As a young man Tolstoy was wild, vain, and reckless. He joined the army in 1851, where he fought in many military campaigns. After leaving the army Tolstoy married, and wrote his two masterpieces, the famous novels *War and Peace* and *Anna Karenina*. Then, in 1879, he suddenly changed. He decided that rich Russians led selfish, empty lives and that he would devote his life to helping the peasants. He even worked and dressed like a peasant. He wrote many religious and moral essays, attacking the unfair Russian system and urging the government to improve the lives of the peasants.

Revolution in 1789 and the execution of the French king in 1793 made Catherine frightened of the ordinary people, and by the end of her reign the serfs were worse off than ever.

The Gap between Rich and Poor

Discontent spread in Russia during the 18th and 19th centuries. While the tsars and rich landowners enjoyed great wealth and luxury, most of the Russian population suffered terrible hardship. Educated Russians formed secret societies that plotted to overthrow the tsars. In 1825 a society called the Decembrists staged an uprising after Tsar Alexander I died. They wanted to stop his son, Nicholas I (ruled 1825–1855), from taking the throne. The rebellion was put down and the rebels were either executed or imprisoned.

Russia's 40 million serfs were freed under Alexander II (ruled 1855–1881). Despite this positive change, discontent was high in Russia. In 1881 Alexander was assassinated by a terrorist bomb. His successor, Alexander III, ruled very harshly. His cruel reign may have been one of the causes of the anger that led to the Russian Revolution early in the 20th century.

Inventions

New Sources of Power

Until the very end of the 17th century all types of machinery and transport relied on the power supplied by wind, water, animals, or humans. Then in 1698 the Englishman Thomas Savery built a steam engine, which was followed in 1712 by another version, built by Thomas Newcomen. It was not until the 1760s when the Scottish engineer James Watt began to improve Newcomen's steam engine that steam was used to power many machines in the factories of the Industrial Revolution. In the early 19th century steam engines also began to be used to power railways and ships. At the very end of the century a new kind of steam engine, the steam turbine, came into use. Its inventor, Charles Parsons, astonished the British navy in 1897 when his boat the *Turbinia,* equipped with a steam turbine engine, reached a speed of 63 kilometres (39 miles) per hour. Many ships were soon equipped with steam turbines, which also began to be used to generate electricity.

The use of electricity for power followed on from the discoveries of the English physicist Michael Faraday. Faraday discovered that moving magnets through a coil of wire produce electricity. This led to both the electrical generator (which he demonstrated in 1831) and the electrical motor. By the end of the 19th century many factory machines were being run on electricity. Electrical lighting also began to

Examples of the first light bulbs, invented by Joseph Swan (left) and Thomas Edison (right).

replace gas lighting, which had been introduced at the beginning of the century. This was made possible by the invention of a long-lasting filament bulb in 1879 by the US inventor Thomas Edison.

A lighter alternative to the steam engine was the internal combustion engine. The first internal combustion engines ran on coal gas, but in the 1880s the German engineers Gottlieb Daimler and Wilhelm Maybach built an internal combustion engine that ran on petrol, which they used in the first four-wheeled car in 1886.

A Revolution in Communications

The 19th century brought a revolution in communications almost as important as the invention of printing. The telegraph, which sends messages down electrical wires using Morse code (a series of long and short signals standing for letters and numbers), was invented in 1837. With the invention of the telephone in 1876 by the Scottish-born Alexander Graham Bell, people could use electrical wires to talk to each other directly, without having to use Morse code. In 1894 the Italian engineer Guglielmo Marconi sent the first radio message, when he sent a signal across his parents' attic that rang a bell on the other side of the room.

The 19th century brought other new ways of communicating. In 1826 the Frenchman Nicéphore Niepce created the first-ever photograph, and many improvements were made to photography over the following

The First Computer

In the 1830s the English mathematician Charles Babbage designed a mechanical calculator called the 'analytical engine'. This is regarded as the forerunner of the modern digital computer. Unfortunately, it was too expensive to build during Babbage's lifetime, although a modern, working replica was made in 1991.

Thomas Edison with a phonograph, one of his many inventions.

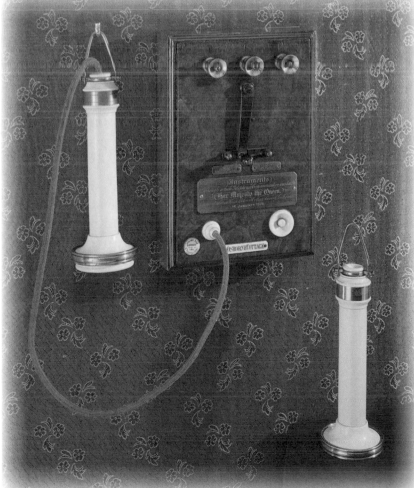

decades. From the 1880s a number of different inventors were trying to make moving pictures – or movies. The first public cinema show was given in Paris in 1895 by two French brothers, August and Louis Lumière using a machine based on one designed by Edison. Films remained silent until 1927, although sound recording itself had been invented in 1877 by Edison. His phonograph system converted the vibrations of sound into wavy grooves on a cylinder. In 1888 cylinders began to be replaced by flat discs called gramophone records, invented by another American, Emile Berliner.

An early example of Alexander Graham Bell's invention, the telephone.

Scientific Discoveries

In the 18th and 19th centuries scientists made important discoveries in many branches of science.

Biology

The Swedish naturalist Carl Linnaeus developed the modern system of classifying living things (putting them into groups depending on similarities). Scientists round the world still use his naming system, in which each species (type) of plant or animal is given a two-word Latin name: for example, humans are *Homo sapiens*.

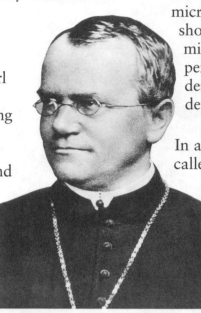
Gregor Mendel, the father of the study of genetics.

The French chemist Louis Pasteur (1822–1895) founded the modern science of microbiology. His work was of great importance in the study of infectious disease. He studied fermentation and discovered that it was caused by living microorganisms, such as yeast, and was not a purely chemical process, as had been thought previously. Pasteur showed that specific kinds of fermentation were caused by specific microorganisms, and that many diseases were also caused by specific germs. Pasteur also put an end to the idea that microbes could simply appear spontaneously, showing that microbes always arise from other microbes. He showed that spoilage of perishable foods could be prevented by destroying microorganisms. This led to the development of the process of pasteurization.

In a monastery garden an Austrian monk called Gregor Mendel (1822–1884) carried out breeding experiments with garden peas that led him to discover the laws of heredity, the way in which characteristics are passed on from one generation to the next. He published his findings in a local natural history society journal in 1866 but the importance of his work was not realized until 1900. His findings laid the foundation for the science of genetics.

Chemistry

In the 18th century chemists tried to find out how and why things burn. After the gas oxygen was discovered, the great French chemist Antoine Lavoisier showed that combustion was the chemical reaction of a substance with oxygen.

The question of what things are actually made of had puzzled people for centuries. In 1803 the British chemist John Dalton came up with the modern definition of the atom: it is the smallest part of an element (such as iron, oxygen, or carbon) that will still behave in the same way in chemical reactions.

The great French scientist Antoine Lavoisier demonstrates one of his discoveries.

In 1897 the British physicist J J Thomson discovered a particle much smaller than the atom – the electron. This was to lead to many astonishing new discoveries in the century that followed, as scientists went on to unravel the secrets of the atom and the terrifying power it contains.

Later in the century the Russian chemist Dmitri Mendeleyev discovered a pattern among all the known elements, and laid them out in what is called the periodic table.

Physics

Important experiments with electricity and magnetism were carried out by the Frenchmen Charles Augustin Coulomb and André Ampère. The Italian Alessandro Volta invented the first practical battery, and the English physicist Michael Faraday discovered how to use moving magnets to generate electricity. The Scottish

Alessandro Volta shows his invention of the first battery to Napoleon.

physicist James Clerk Maxwell then suggested the idea of an electromagnetic force, which would be present in various types of wave, including light. Later in the century other types of electromagnetic waves were discovered, such as radio waves and X-rays.

Other physicists in the 19th century studied heat and energy – the science of thermodynamics. Among them were the English brewery owner James Joule and the Scottish physicist Lord Kelvin. They showed that heat is a type of energy, and that energy cannot be created or destroyed. It can, however, change from one form into another, for example a steam engine turns heat energy into mechanical energy.

The astronomer William Herschel wih his sister Caroline, herself an accomplished astronomer.

New Planets

In 1781 the amateur astronomer Sir William Herschel came across a new object in the sky, which turned out to be a planet – Uranus. This was the first new planet to be discovered since ancient times. Some 60 years later two mathematicians independently worked out that there must be another unknown planet, and predicted where it would be. The planet, Neptune, was found in 1846.

Darwin and His Theory of Evolution

In Victorian times most people in Europe and the USA were Christians. They believed in the Bible, which said that God created the world and everything in it in seven days. However, some people already had their doubts about this.

Geologists – scientists who study the planet Earth – showed that the Earth was older than the Bible said. Fossils showed that some animals and plants had become extinct (died out). The fact that there were living animals that looked similar to others that were extinct led some people to suggest that living things changed, or evolved, over time, giving rise to new species (types) of plants and animals. This idea was upsetting to those who believed that God had created everything.

A fossil Archaeopteryx, a reptile that shows some of the features of a bird.

The Galápagos Islands

Darwin made his most important discoveries when he sailed on a scientific voyage to South America on HMS *Beagle* between 1831 and 1836. He noticed that many of the animals on the Galápagos Islands, about 1,000 kilometres (620 miles) to the west of the South American mainland, were similar to those on the mainland, but not the same. Also, he realized that closely related animals lived on different islands.

Darwin studied different species of finch (a small bird) living on different islands. He noticed that they fed on different foods. For example, one finch could hold a cactus spine in its beak and use it to take grubs from holes in logs. Another had a small, slender beak for eating small insects. On a different island the finches had strong, stout beaks for crushing seeds. Darwin concluded that all the Galápagos finches were descended from the same older type of finch. Over time its beak had adapted to the type of food it found in different environments.

A seal is a mammal that has become adapted to life in the water.

Darwin's Theory of Natural Selection

The English naturalist Charles Darwin put forward a theory that species evolve from other species through a process that he named 'natural selection'.

He developed his theory after noticing that the individual animals in a species are all slightly different. Some are slightly better adapted, or suited, to the environment they live in. Darwin said that the ones that are better adapted are more likely to survive and breed than those that are less well adapted. Gradually, over time, the features of better adapted animals are passed down the generations, becoming common within a population.

The Impact of Darwin's Theory

While Darwin was working on a book about his theory he found that Alfred Russel Wallace had come up with the same idea. Darwin never tried to claim the idea for himself. He published his book *On the Origin of Species* in 1859. It had a huge impact. Although the book did not say anything about humans, it was obvious from his work that he thought they had also evolved from earlier species. Many people were horrified to hear the idea that over many millions of years humans had evolved from apes, as humans had supposedly been created in God's own image. Some scientists agreed with Darwin, but others did not, and debate raged around Europe and the USA. There are still debates about Darwin's theory today, but it is now largely accepted as true.

Charles Darwin (1809–1882)

Charles Darwin was born in Shrewsbury, England, in 1809. Although he studied to become a clergyman in the Church of England, he became more interested in natural history. In 1831 he set off on the British naval ship HMS *Beagle* to study geology and biology in South America. Later he lived in London and Kent.

Darwin suffered greatly from ill-health. He was very worried about his discoveries concerning evolution and the effect they would have on society. After *On the Origin of Species* was published, he did not become very involved in defending his theory, although he continued his research. In 1871 he published *The Descent of Man and Selection in Relation to Sex*, which showed that humans had evolved from apes. After publishing this book he concentrated on studying plants.

South Africa: the Afrikaners, the British, and the Africans

The Peoples of Southern Africa

In 1652 the Dutch founded a colony on the Cape of Good Hope at the tip of southern Africa. The first people who met them were the San (Bushmen) and the Khoikhoi (Hottentots), known together as the Khoisan. They were hunters and gatherers who later settled down to grow crops and keep cattle. Among many other peoples to the east were the Xhosa, and to the northeast were the Zulus. The Dutch took the Khoisan as slaves.

The Great Trek

Britain took the Cape from the Dutch in 1814, and soon afterwards English-speaking people settled there, fighting the Xhosa people in the east for more land. Many of the Dutch – who became known as Boers (farmers) or Afrikaners – were unhappy with British rule, and in 1836 they loaded all their belongings into ox-wagons and began a great trek north, taking 600 slaves with them. The Great Trek is a very important event in Afrikaner history.

The Great Trek of the Boers to escape British rule.

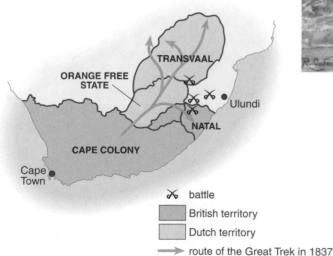

Shaka Zulu and the *Mfecane*

The Zulus, led by King Shaka, had created chaos among African peoples. Their *Mfecane* ('crushing') of weaker neighbours in order to find new land for themselves had turned many people into homeless and hungry refugees. Much of the land seemed empty when the Boers arrived. Some of the trekkers, including women and children, were killed by Zulus led

by Shaka's successor Dingane. The Boers got their revenge at the Battle of Blood River in 1838, when they killed 3,000 Zulus with a force of 500 men. The Boers went on to found the independent republics of the Orange Free State and Transvaal.

Famous Battles

Fighting continued between the Boers and the Zulus, the Zulus and the British, and the British and the Boers. In the Zulu War of 1879 the Zulus defeated the British at the Battle of

British and Boer troops fight in one of the battles of the Second Boer War.

Isandlwana, killing 1,600 British soldiers using only spears and shields. However, a few months later the British took the Zulu capital of Ulundi and won the war.

The discovery of diamonds in 1871 and gold in 1886 in the Transvaal increased the bitterness between the two white nations. The British attempt to take the Transvaal in the First Anglo-Boer War ended in a humiliating defeat at Majuba in 1881.

The Second Anglo-Boer War

The British badly wanted to control the diamond and gold mines, and in 1899 the Second Anglo-Boer War, or South African War, broke out. The Afrikaners won several of the early battles, such as Spion Kop, but the British won the war and took over their land in 1902. During the war a British soldier, Sir Alfred Milner, invented concentration camps, in which many Afrikaner women and children died.

Shaka Zulu (about 1787–1828)

Shaka Zulu was a great military leader who reorganized the Zulu army. He replaced their long throwing spears with short ones for close fighting, and also introduced long shields. His army consisted of well-organized young warriors who lived in a barracks and wore no shoes so that they could run faster. Even without guns, Zulu armies using Shaka's tactics managed to beat both Boer and British armies. Shaka was killed by his half-brother Dingane.

China and the West

In 1644 a peasant rebellion brought an end to the Ming dynasty (line of emperors) that had ruled China for nearly 300 years. In the confusion, non-Chinese nomads (people who do not settle in one place) from Manchuria took control of northern China, and set up a new dynasty known as the Manchu, or Qing, dynasty. Civil war continued in the south, but by 1682 the Manchu had established their rule over the whole of China.

At first China prospered under the Manchu, but in the 18th century the Manchu's policy of isolation, in which the rulers stopped China from trading with other countries, weakened China's position in the world. A series of wars and natural disasters in the 19th century resulted in the Manchu rulers losing even more power. At the end of the century it appeared as if the whole country of China would be divided up and ruled by the USA and the main European powers.

The Opium Wars

In the 19th century Britain sold an addictive drug called opium to many people in China. Although this was illegal, dishonest merchants and corrupt officials made it impossible for the government to stop its sale. In 1839 the Chinese government had had enough. It sent the commissioner Lin Zexu to the port of Guangzhou (Canton) where he confiscated and destroyed 20,000 chests of British opium. This sparked off the first Opium War in 1839. By 1842 the Manchu government was utterly defeated, and China was forced to open five ports to foreign trade and surrender Hong Kong to Britain. The Chinese were again defeated in a second Opium War (1856–1860), which ended with an Anglo–French army occupying the capital, Beijing.

The British ship *Nemesis* sinks Chinese war junks during the Opium Wars.

The signing of the Treaty of Nanking in 1842, which gave Hong Kong to Britain.

The Taiping Rebellion (1850–1864)

In addition to all the defeats its army had suffered in battle, in the mid-19th century China suffered a series of natural disasters, including famines, droughts, and floods. The people grew increasingly dissatisfied with the weak Qing dynasty, which did little to help them. Anger was especially high in the south. It was here that a village teacher, Hong Xiuquan, started the Taiping Rebellion. Hong and his followers wanted a China where the peasants owned and worked the land, and men and women were equal. The government raised an army to crush the rebellion, but the rebels formed themselves into highly disciplined armies. It took 14 years, and the help of British and French forces, to finally defeat them. This was the largest uprising in modern Chinese history, leaving a reported 20 million people dead.

The Taiping Rebellion was a popular uprising that took several years to defeat.

Further Decline

The power of the Manchu continued to decline throughout the 19th century. Countries such as Britain, France, Germany, and the USA gained control of many Chinese ports, and ruled them as their own. Russia was expanding on China's western and northern borders, and in a war from 1894 to 1895 Japan seized the Chinese possessions of Korea and Taiwan. Towards the end of the century various Chinese leaders formed the 'Self-Strengthening Movement' in an effort to westernize China and stop it from losing all its power. The government set about modernizing education, the army, industry, transport, and communications. However, this attempt to come to terms with the modern world and the West was resisted by the powerful mother of the emperor, the dowager empress Tz'u-hsi, who was the real ruler of China from 1861 until her death in 1908.

In 1900 the dowager gave her backing to the anti-Western 'Boxer' rebels. These rebels, led by a militia unit called the Fists of Righteous Harmony, tried to rid China of Western influence. They killed a number of foreigners and marched on Beijing, where they besieged the foreign embassies. Western forces entered the city and crushed the rebellion. The following year they forced the Chinese to agree to another humiliating peace, which demanded money from China and the right for foreign troops to be stationed on Chinese soil.

Japan: A Growing Power

After 1639 Japan had a 'closed door' policy. This meant the Japanese government put strict controls on who could enter or leave Japan. The only foreigners allowed into Japan were a few Dutch and Chinese traders, who were restricted to the port of Nagasaki. The penalty for any Japanese attempting to leave the country was death. In 1853 and 1854 Commodore Matthew Perry forced Japan to open two of its ports to US trade. Trade relationships with other nations, such as Britain and Russia, followed.

Emperor Meiji and his family.

Japanese women spinning silk thread.

Japan's links with outsiders weakened the power of the *shoguns*. The *shoguns* were military leaders who had ruled Japan for centuries, while the emperors remained powerless. The *shoguns* were replaced by a return to imperial government in 1868. The Emperor Meiji, who gave his name to the period, thoroughly modernized Japan and began its transformation into a world power.

Industrialization

Japan was one of the very few Asian countries not colonized by the West. The main reason for this was because it rapidly became a powerful industrial nation. The Japanese sent their students abroad to study in European and American universities, and invited Western

Silk

By modernizing its methods of silk production, Japan was able to produce a large proportion of all the world's silk in the late 19th century. Silk is made from the continuous filaments a silkworm uses to spin its cocoon. The filaments are unwound from several cocoons and then twisted to form a single, thin strand. Several of these strands are twisted together to make a stronger strand. This process is called 'throwing'.

industrialists, engineers, and soldiers to Japan to advise on the modernization process.

Industrialization began in 1873 when the old feudal system which had controlled people's lives was abolished and new political, economic, and social systems were put into place. The Bank of Japan was established and the government poured money into building railways, factories, and telegraph lines. Coal mines, steel mills, and shipyards were set up by Japanese businessmen. Factories for silk and other products such as glass and clothing were opened. In just over 30 years these changes made Japan a strong economic power.

Education

During the Meiji period education became compulsory (required by law), and by the end of the 19th century nearly all Japanese children attended school. The Japanese schools were organized in the same way as French and German schools.

Inside a factory for making boots.

Military Power

The Meiji ambition to modernize Japan included reorganizing the army. In 1870 the government set up an imperial army, which soon became as well-equipped and efficient as any of the armies in Europe. With such a strong military force, Japan began to look outside its own borders for new territory to colonize. Its first step was to take control of the neighbouring islands of Hokkaido, Ryukyu, Kuril, and Bonin. Successful wars with China in 1894 to 1895 and Russia in 1904 to 1905 resulted in Japan taking Korea, Taiwan, southern Manchuria, and half of Sakhalin.

A woodblock print showing various forms of transport in Japan.

The Iwakura Mission

In 1871 the influential politician Iwakura Tomomi was appointed to take a group of Japanese officials on a fact-finding trip to the West. Officially, the purpose of the trip was to revise treaties, but it was actually a great learning mission. The 50 members of the group divided into teams to study all aspects of Western culture, including education, mining, medicine, science, and law. The Iwakura Mission published its findings in five volumes.

In the 1870s the Japanese were fascinated by Western culture. At first they invited foreign experts to teach them how to make Western art and clothing, write Western literature, and think Western thoughts. Later they combined ideas from the West with their own traditional values.

The Rise of Big Business

In the late 19th century some American entrepreneurs turned the Industrial Revolution into big business. Efficiency was important to them and they were quick to see the advantages of modern, large-scale factories and mass-production techniques. They wanted control over every part of their industries. The owner of Standard Oil, John D Rockefeller, is one example. By the late 1870s he had taken over nearly all the small oil wells and refineries in the USA. Then he took control of the railways that transported the oil to market. He made his own barrels and oil lamps. Finally, he bought out the retailers and sold the oil himself.

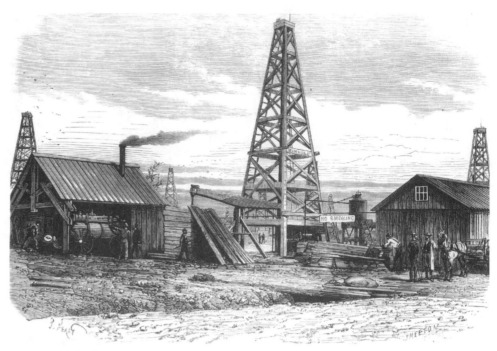

Oil Creek in Pennsylvania, one of the earliest oil fields in the United States.

Methods like Rockefeller's were very successful and earned enormous fortunes. The industrialists used some of the money to make the USA more productive. Their profits financed the railway and shipping industries, the telegraph and telephone, the new electrical industry, and steel. But many people detested the industrialists for getting so rich while life was still hard for their workers. The railway millionaire William Vanderbilt was not concerned. His response was 'The public be damned!'

Workers stoking the boilers in an oil refinery in 1880.

The Richest Man in the World

Andrew Carnegie (1835–1919) was born in Dunfermline, Scotland, the son of a poor weaver. When his family emigrated to the USA in 1848, he was determined to bring his family out of poverty. By the time he was 33, Carnegie was worth $400,000 (about £8 million today). In the 1870s he turned his attention to steel. By holding down costs, driving his workforce hard, and using the latest technology, his company, Carnegie Steel, sold the best and cheapest steel available. By 1900 Carnegie Steel produced more steel than the entire British steel industry. When the company was sold to the powerful banker J P Morgan in 1901, Andrew Carnegie earned $250 million (about £7.5 billion today).

Levi Strauss (1829–1902)

The first jeans were invented in 1873 by Levi Strauss. Born in Bavaria, in Germany, in 1829, Strauss sailed to New York when he was 18 years old. In 1850 he headed west to sell goods to the miners looking for gold in California. They needed sturdy, hard-wearing trousers so Strauss hired the tailor Jacob Davis to make waist overalls, now called jeans, using tent canvas. Later denim was substituted and copper rivets (pins) were added to the pocket seams to make them even stronger. The 'Levis' were a great success and Strauss died a wealthy man in 1902.

Department Stores

Department stores sold a variety of goods in separate departments, each with its own manager. The Bon Marché in Paris became the first department store in the world in about 1865. One of the most famous department stores, Harrods of London, began as a small grocery store in 1849. Its owner, Henry Charles Harrod, added many new departments in the late 19th century, including a gourmet food hall.

The Great Exhibition

In 1849 Queen Victoria's husband, Prince Albert, thought up the idea of a great exhibition where people could come to see the wonders of the industrial age. The iron and glass Crystal Palace was built to house the exhibits, and the Great Exhibition opened two years later in Hyde Park, London. There were 14,000 exhibitors showing everything from false teeth and artificial legs to the Colt repeating pistol. Over 6 million people attended the exhibition.

The glove counter in the Bon Marché department store, Paris, in 1880.

Mail-Order Shopping

Americans unable to visit the smart city department stores were offered an attractive alternative – mail order. The most famous mail-order operation was Sears, Roebuck and Company. It was founded in 1887 to sell watches and jewellery by mail, but by 1893 its 300-page catalogue offered everything from fur coats to kitchen appliances and farm implements.

Sport: The Origins of Football and Rugby

Ball Games

Ball games have been played for a very long time and probably began by people throwing fruit or balls of grass to each other. Games with sticks or bats, the ancestors of hockey and cricket may, have been played with animal bones or bits of wood. Sport was often used to train soldiers for battle. The Chinese army played a kind of football 1,500 years ago in which they used the head of an enemy as a ball. Native American warriors played lacrosse (*baggataway*) as part of their training.

Blackburn Rovers playing Notts County in an FA Challenge Cup match in 1891.

Association Football

In medieval England football was played at fairs and on holidays with the stomach or bladder of an animal blown up like a balloon. There was no marked field and hundreds of people might play at one time, running through the streets chasing a pig's bladder.

Football was introduced to British schools in the mid-19th century and rules made up to make the game safer. Each team had to have the same number of players, and referees were brought in to stop games getting too rough. Soccer, rugby, and American football all came from this game.

The rules of football were drawn up by the London Football Association in 1863. The first international match, between England and Scotland, was played in 1872, and the first full-time league was started in 1888. Soccer (the name comes from 'association') was taken all over the world by British sailors and settlers, and it became popular wherever it was played. Players in the 19th century wore heavy leather boots with studs nailed to their soles. Each player wore a different outfit so it was sometimes hard for spectators to know who belonged to which side.

The first football game to be played between Harvard and Yale universities in 1875.

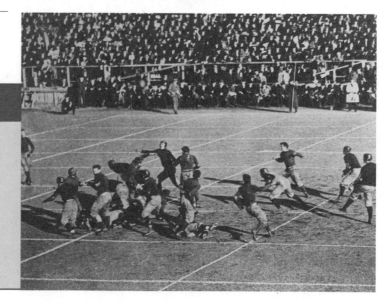

American Football

American football was first played in 1869 between the universities of Rutgers and Princeton in New Jersey, USA. It was a dangerous and very physical game using an oval ball. There were 25 players on each side. In 1876 teams were reduced to 11 players who did not wear much protective clothing. In 1905, 18 college footballers died and 150 were badly injured. This led to rule changes to make the game safer and the introduction of new padded clothing.

Rugby as it was played at Rugby School around 1870.

Rugby

Rugby is said to have been invented at Rugby School in 1823 when William Webb Ellis, picked up a football and ran with it. Rugby was played by two teams of 15 players on a field with two H-shaped goals. The ball, which is oval, rather than round as in football, can be kicked or carried but must only be thrown backwards. The first Rugby Union was founded in London in 1871.

In 1895 22 clubs in northern England called for their players to be compensated for the wages they lost by turning out to play on Saturday. This led to the introduction of Rugby Union and a new game called Rugby League in which there were 13 professional (paid) players in a team, and different rules. Rugby Union, which stayed completely amateur (unpaid) until recently, is much more widely played throughout the world.

The Rugby Union World Cup is a competition for the William Webb Ellis trophy, and was first held in 1987. The Rugby League World Cup was first held in 1954.

Sport: Bats, Sticks, and Rackets

Cricket

Cricket in the 18th century was played with five players in each team. There was only one wicket, which had two stumps instead of three. The first code of cricket laws was written in 1744. Lord's Cricket Ground in London, founded by Thomas Lord in 1787, is known as the 'home of cricket'. In the 1800s the British introduced cricket to their colonies and it is still played in India, Pakistan, Sri Lanka, Australia, the West Indies, and South Africa.

What has become known as the first Test Match between national teams was played between England and Australia in 1877. The Australians won by 45 runs. The first women's Test Match, which England won easily, was played in Adelaide, Australia, in 1934. Women had always played cricket, and in fact roundarm bowling was introduced by a

A cricket match at Lord's in 1837.

woman, Christina Willes of Kent, in the early 19th century, to avoid the ball being lost in her full skirts. Her invention was added to the laws in 1835 and started the transition from underarm to the overarm bowling that is used today. The first official women's cricket team in England was founded in 1887 and lasted until 1951.

W G Grace, probably the most famous English cricketer, played for the all-England eleven at the age of 15. All he knew about cricket had been taught to him by his mother in the family orchard where she coached all her sons. In his first class career between 1865 and 1908, he scored 54,896 runs and took 2,876 wickets.

W G Grace, one of England's greatest cricketers.

Boxing

In the 18th and 19th centuries boxing was a bare-knuckle prize-fight which could go on as long as six hours – until one or both of the fighters were totally exhausted. It was sponsored by rich men who gambled on the fighters. The cruelty of the sport meant that it was eventually stopped. Modern boxing began with a code of rules supported by the Marquess of Queensbury in 1866. The code made boxers wear padded gloves, said that rounds should only last three minutes, and said that there must be a referee.

Baseball

Baseball is North America's national sport and is very similar to the British game rounders, which was brought to America by the settlers in the 1700s. In 1845 the Knickerbocker Baseball Club of New York drew up the rules that established the modern nine-player team and the four-base diamond. The first organised league, the National Association of Baseball Players, was established in 1858.

The Wimbledon tennis championship semi-final match in 1881.

Racket Sports

Real or royal tennis was played indoors and was popular in later medieval and Renaissance Europe. In the 19th century lawn tennis was developed in England by Major Walter C Wingfield. It quickly became popular as a game for both men and women. Rackets were wooden with pear-shaped heads strung loosely. The first world championship was played at Wimbledon, England, in 1877.

The only game to be invented in a prison was rackets. It was first played in Fleet Prison, London, in the 18th century, where prisoners started hitting a ball against a wall to pass the time. It was played a century later at Harrow School, and it was there that squash was invented, a similar game played with a 'squashy' rubber ball.

Index

Picture Acknowledgements

t = top, b = bottom, l = left, r = right, c = centre

5 t AKG London b, Victoria and Albert Museum, London/Bridgeman Art Library; 6 The Royal Institution, London/Bridgeman Art Library; 7 t Bibliothèque Nationale, Paris/Erich Lessing/AKG London, b Musée Carnavalet, Paris/Giraudon/Bridgeman Art Library; 8 Mary Evans Picture Library; 9 t Science Museum/Science and Society Picture Library, b Private Collection/Bridgeman Art Library; 10 Metropolitan Museum of Art, New York/Bridgeman Art Library; 11 Private Collection/Bridgeman Art Library; 12 Musée Carnavalet, Paris/Bulloz/Bridgeman Art Library; 13 t Musée Carnavalet, Paris/et archive, b Musée Carnavalet, Paris/Giraudon/Bridgeman Art Library; 14 l Musée des Beaux-Arts, Lille/ Giraudon/Bridgeman Art Library, r Corbis; 16–17 Private Collection/Stapleton Collection/Bridgeman Art Library; 18 Museum of the City of New York/Bridgeman Art Library; 19 t Mary Evans Picture Library, b National Motor Museum, Beaulieu; 20 Waterways Museum, Stoke Bruerne/et archive; 21 t Private Collection/Bridgeman Art Library, b The Illustrated London News Picture Library/Bridgeman Art Library; 22 Mary Evans Picture Library; 23 t Stapleton Collection/Bridgeman Art Library, b Mary Evans Picture Library; 24 t Beaford Centre/et archive; 25 t Science Museum/Science and Society Picture Library, b et archive; 26 t Musée de Val de Grace/et archive, b Jean-Loup Charmet/Science Photo Library; 27 Port Royal, Paris/et archive; 28 Wolverhampton Art Gallery, West Midlands/Bridgeman Art Library; 29 t Chris Beetles Ltd, London/Bridgeman Art Library, c Christie's Images, b Wolverhampton Art Gallery, West Midlands/Bridgeman Art Library; 30 Mary Evans Picture Library; 31 Private Collection/ Bridgeman Art Library; 32 t et archive, b Yuri Lewinski/Collections; 33 John Miller/Collections; 34 t British Library, London/Bridgeman Art Library, b Private Collection/Bridgeman Art Library; 35 Musée d'Orsay, Paris/Bridgeman Art Library; 36 et archive; 37 t Mansell Time Inc, b Mary Evans Picture Library; 38 Bibliothèque Nationale, Paris/Lauros-Giraudon/Bridgeman Art Library; 39–40 Private Collection/Bridgeman Art Library; 41 t AKG London, b Mary Evans Picture Library; 42 l The Science Museum/Science and Society Picture Library, r Mary Evans Picture Library; 43 Private Collection/Bridgeman Art Library; 44 t Royal Holloway and New Bedford College, Surrey/Bridgeman Art Library, b AKG London; 45 Scottish National Portrait Gallery, Edinburgh/Bridgeman Art Library; 46 et archive; 47 Victoria Art Gallery, Bath and North East Somerset Council/Bridgeman Art Library; 48 et archive; 49 t Corbis/Bettmann, b Private Collection/Bridgeman; 50 AKG London; 51 t Library of Congress, b Yale Univercity/et archive; 52 Private Collection/Stapleton Collection/Bridgeman Art Library; 53 t NMPFT/Science and Society Picture Library, b AKG London; 54 AKG London; 55 British Library, London/Bridgeman Art Library; 57 l et archive, r Mary Evans Picture Library; 58 Museum of African and Oceanic Art, Paris/et archive; 59 t British Museum/et archive, b et archive; 60–61 Mary Evans Picture Library; 62 Trustees of the Watts Gallery, Compton, Surrey/Bridgeman Art Library; 63 Private Collection/Bridgeman Art Library; 64 t Mary Evans Picture Library, b Private Collection/ Bridgeman Art Library; 65 Mary Evans Picture Library; 66 Royal Geographical Society/AKG London; 67 et archive; 69 t Palazzo Publico, Siena/Bridgeman Art Library, b Private Collection/Bridgeman Art Library; 70 Hermitage, St. Petersburg/Bridgeman Art Library; 71 Tretyakov Gallery, Moscow/Bridgeman Art Library; 72 Science Museum/Science and Society Picture Library; 73 t AKG London, b Science Museum/Science and Society Picture Library; 74–75 Mary Evans Picture; 76 Natural History Museum, London; 77 l Doug Allan/Oxford Scientific Films, r Down House, Downe, Kent/Bridgeman Art Library; 78 Mary Evans Picture Library; 79 et archive; 80 et archive; 81 t National Maritime Museum, b School of Oriental and African Studies/et archive; 82 t AKG London, 82 b–83 t et archive; 83 b National Railway Museum/Science and Society Picture Library; 84–85 Mary Evans Picture Library; 86 t Mary Evans Picture Libray, b Corbis; 87 Mary Evans Picture Library; 88 t Marylebone Library, London/ Bridgeman Art Library, b Marylebone Cricket Club, London/Bridgeman Art Library; 89 Mary Evans Picture Library.

Cover illustrations (clockwise from top right):
National Railway Museum/Science & Society; Christie's Images; Corbis; Mary Evans Picture Library; British Museum/et archive,

Every effort has been made to give the correct acknowledgement for each picture. However, should there be any inaccuracy or omission, we would be pleased to insert the correct acknowledgement in a future edition or printing of this volume.